CHEROKEE

APR 1 1 1993

The Land and People of

CANADA

The Land and People of®
CANADA

by Andrew H. Malcolm

HarperCollins*Publishers*

Portions of this text appeared in a different form in Andrew H. Malcolm's *The Canadians* (Times Books, 1985). Used by permission.

Country maps by Joe LeMonnier
Photo research by Rod Beebe
Every effort has been made to locate the copyright holders of all copyrighted material and secure the necessary permission to reproduce them. In the event of any questions arising as to their use, the publisher will be glad to make necessary changes in future printings and editions.
The map on page 79 is based on a map from *The Canadian Encyclopedia* © 1988 by Hurtig Publishers Ltd., Canada.

THE LAND AND PEOPLE OF
is a registered trademark of
HarperCollins Publishers.
The Land and People of Canada
Copyright © 1991 by Unlimited Words, Ltd., Andrew H. Malcolm
Printed in the U.S.A. All rights reserved.
For information address HarperCollins Children's Books, a division of HarperCollins Publishers, 10 East 53rd Street, New York, NY 10022

Library of Congress Cataloging-in-Publication Data
Malcolm, Andrew H., date
    The land and people of Canada / by Andrew Malcolm.
        p.   cm. — (Portraits of the nations)
    Includes bibliographical references and index.
    Includes filmography: p.
    Includes discography: p.
    Summary: Introduces the history, geography, people, culture, government, and economy of Canada.
        ISBN 0-06-022494-0. — ISBN 0-06-022495-9 (lib. bdg.)
        1. Canada—Juvenile literature.   [1. Canada.]   I. Title.
    II. Series.
    F1008.2.M29   1991   90-47560
    971—dc20   CIP
                                                                    AC

1   2   3   4   5   6   7   8   9   10
First Edition

Contents

THE WORLD

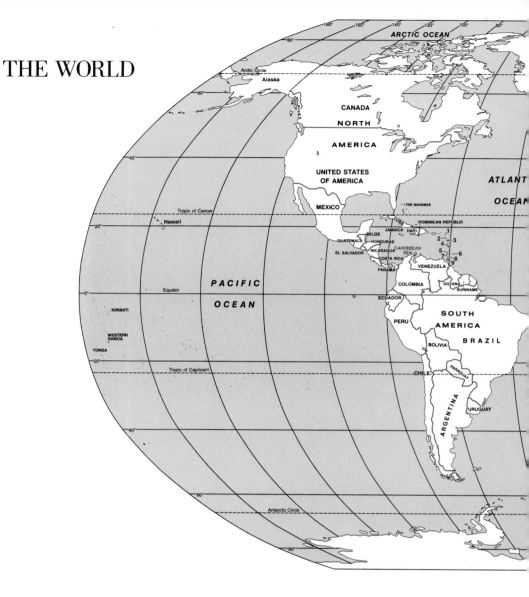

This world map is based on a projection developed by Arthur H. Robinson. The shape of each country and its size, relative to other countries, are more accurately expressed here than in previous maps. The map also gives equal importance to all of the continents, instead of placing North America at the center of the world. *Used by permission of the Foreign Policy Association.*

Legend

——— International boundaries

--------- Disputed or undefined boundaries

Projection: Robinson

| 0 | 1000 | 2000 | 3000 Miles |
| 0 | 1000 | 2000 | 3000 Kilometers |

Caribbean Nations

1. Anguilla
2. St. Christopher and Nevis
3. Antigua and Barbuda
4. Dominica
5. St. Lucia
6. Barbados
7. St. Vincent
8. Grenada
9. Trinidad and Tobago

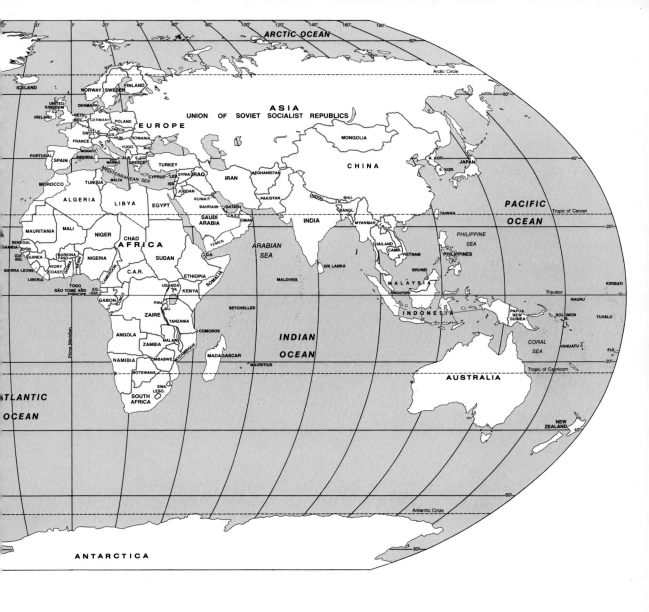

Abbreviations

ALB.	—Albania	C.A.R.	—Central African Republic	LEB.	—Lebanon	SWA.	—Swaziland
AUS.	—Austria	CZECH.	—Czechoslovakia	LESO.	—Lesotho	SWITZ.	—Switzerland
BANGL.	—Bangladesh	DJI.	—Djibouti	LIE.	—Liechtenstein	U.A.E.	—United Arab Emirates
BEL.	—Belgium	EQ. GUI.	—Equatorial Guinea	LUX.	—Luxemburg	YUGO.	—Yugoslavia
BHU.	—Bhutan	GER.	Germany	NETH.	—Netherlands		
BU.	—Burundi	GUI. BIS.	—Guinea Bissau	N. KOR.	—North Korea		
BUL.	—Bulgaria	HUN.	—Hungary	RWA.	—Rwanda		
CAMB.	—Cambodia	ISR.	—Israel	S. KOR.	—South Korea		

Mini Facts

OFFICIAL NAME: Canada

LOCATION: North America, with Alaska (U.S.) and the Pacific Ocean forming the western boundary and the Atlantic Ocean the eastern; the United States borders the country to the south, the Arctic Ocean borders it to the north.

AREA: 3,851,809 square miles (9,976,185 square kilometers)

CAPITAL: Ottawa

POPULATION: 26,584,064 (Statistics of Canada, 1990 Official Estimate)

OFFICIAL LANGUAGES: English, French

RELIGIONS: Roman Catholic (47.3%); Protestant (41.2%); no preference (7.4%); Eastern Orthodox (1.5%); Jewish (1.2%) (Statistics of Canada, 1981 Census)

TYPE OF GOVERNMENT: Confederation, with parliamentary democracy

HEAD OF STATE: Monarch of Great Britain and British Commonwealth

HEAD OF GOVERNMENT: Prime Minister (Brian Mulroney, head of Progressive Conservative party)

PARLIAMENT: Constitutionally made up of House of Commons, Senate, and ruling monarch; in common usage, made up of House of Commons and Senate

ADULT LITERACY: 99%

LIFE EXPECTANCY: Female, 79.8; Male, 72.9

MAIN PRODUCTS: *Manufacturing*—transportation equipment, petroleum, chemicals, wood products
Agricultural—wheat, barley, oats, livestock
Mining—nickel, zinc, copper, gold, lead, molybdenum, potash, silver

CURRENCY: Canadian dollar. Conversion rates with U.S. dollars vary; U.S. dollars are used in this book.

Foreword

No two countries in the world are more important to each other than Canada and the United States.

Together, they have shared a common colonial parent, a common continent, a common language, a common border free of geographical barriers, and a democratic heritage; and, increasingly, their 270 million combined citizens share an integrated economy. Thousands of Canadians and Americans live in each other's countries. Millions of Americans travel to Canada each year. Millions of Canadians return the visit, most often during the winter, when in Florida alone one eighth of the population is sun-seeking Canadians.

Canadians and Americans own vast amounts of each other's land and corporations. Their police are linked by common computers. They watch each other's television programs without notice. Canadian officers routinely work in the most-secret Colorado mountain hideout of America's air-defense system. Canadians and Americans even share the same professional baseball and hockey leagues. Although they have twice fought each other, not since long before Canada's confederation in 1867 have these cousin-countries exchanged anything more lethal than annoyance.

Yet for two countries that share so much, including vast stakes in each other's stability and success, Canadians and Americans both remain woefully ignorant of each other. Like a couple peacefully married for decades, both countries have come to take the other for granted,

Horseshoe Falls at Niagara Falls. Canada is on the left side of the picture, the United States on the right. Government of Canada, ISTC

planting the silent seeds for disastrous future misunderstandings and suspicions. It is much harder, but no less necessary, to work at a relationship that seems so natural and easy than at one that seems more obviously foreign. People can accept foreigners not knowing their ways, but not family.

As the child of two Canadians, I had grown up in Canada and later lived in the United States, and my family's life constantly straddled the border. With friends, relatives, homes, and even stamp collections, toys, and pets in Canada and the United States, I was a dual citizen and always felt part of both lands but all of neither.

That provided a unique perspective when for several years I was assigned to cover Canada as the Toronto Bureau Chief for *The New York Times.* I crossed the country countless times on planes, on trains, and in cars. I wandered through its tidy streets and plush corporate board-rooms, its mines and villages, its woods and wilderness alleys. I drifted down Canada's rivers, followed its migrating whales and caribou, and hiked across the Arctic Circle. I landed on the polar ice pack, spent days in Indian dogsleds and tents, and went on snowmobile patrol with the Mounties. I interviewed Canada's business executives, politicians, and mechanics, its immigrants, actors, athletes, and natives, its students, housewives, musicians, chefs, and writers. I even found the old field-stone hut, now crumbling beneath old age and the prairie winds, where my father had grown up, milking cows and walking to a one-room schoolhouse.

This is the very personal story of that fascinating journey, and of some of the discoveries and friendships I made along the way. Those years gave me valuable insights into how much both peoples have in common and in contrast. And how important it is for both country's voters, present and future, to understand each other better and to work harder at building a lasting amicable relationship as our two lands inevitably grow ever closer. That takes durable goodwill and diligence on both sides. As President John F. Kennedy once told a Canadian audience, "Geography made us neighbors. History made us friends. And economics has made us partners."

—Andrew H. Malcolm

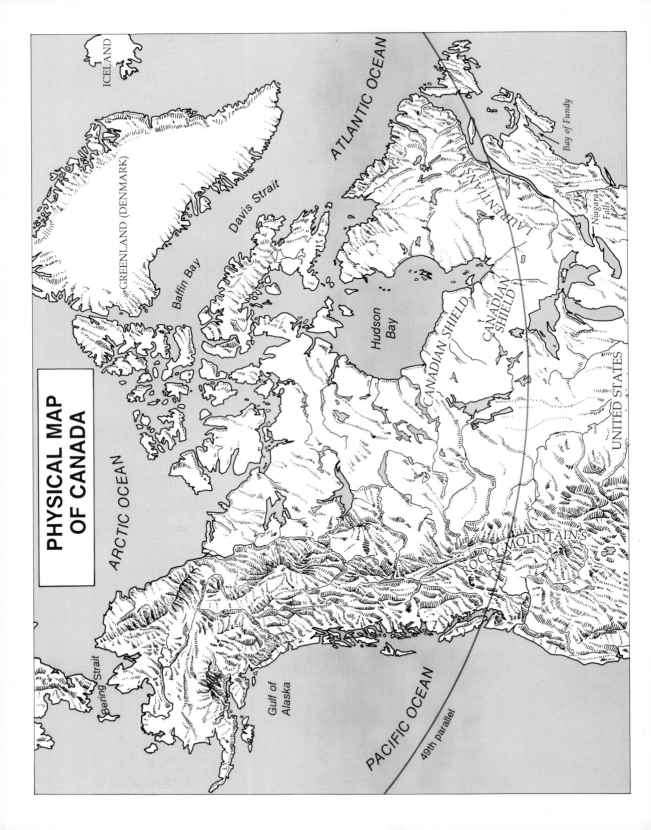

PHYSICAL MAP OF CANADA

ICELAND

ATLANTIC OCEAN

GREENLAND (DENMARK)

Davis Strait

Baffin Bay

LAURENTIANS

Bay of Fundy

Niagara Falls

Hudson Bay

CANADIAN SHIELD

CANADIAN SHIELD

ARCTIC OCEAN

UNITED STATES

ROCKY MOUNTAINS

Bering Strait

Gulf of Alaska

PACIFIC OCEAN

49th parallel

Geography: A Land Lost in Itself

About a hundred parents had gathered in the tiny school auditorium one evening in Toronto when their fourth-grade youngsters raised the curtain on a homemade cardboard stage. The evening's show, using puppets made by the students and a script they wrote themselves too, began with a puppet interviewing the finalists in a beauty show.

"My name is Betty Lou Jones," said the first contestant in a fake American Southern accent, "and I'm from Durham, North Carolina."

"My name is Betty Sue Barker," said the next young lady puppet, "and I'm from Little Rock, Arkansas."

The last puppet finalist spoke very softly, and the chuckling parents leaned forward to listen. "My name is Roberta Mackenzie, and I'm from Canada," she said. "But I don't know what that is."

The retractable skydome in Toronto allows teams like the Blue Jays and Argonauts to play in any weather.   Canapress Photo Service

The immediate, knowing outburst of parental laughter ignited prolonged applause that required extra bows all around. Somehow, with their natural openness and honesty, those nine-year-olds had struck a key chord in the Canadian personality. Statistics can show where Canadians come from, where they live now, when they marry, give birth and die, and how they earn a living and spend their time and money.

But after more than 365 years of European settlement and a century and a quarter of independence as a dominion, no one—least of all Canadians themselves—has been able to tell Canadians who they are. Those Canadians moved by such debates have always found it easy to declare fervently that they are not Americans or Yankees. Living in the shadows of the world's two largest superpowers—the United States and the Soviet Union—it has proven much harder for those Canadians to define a positive identity, although few would deny there is one.

For Americans, perhaps the most surprising single discovery about Canada is that a land so rich in so many ways, still so pure in so many places, with a people so obviously intelligent, hardy, warm, innocent, and insistent on who they are *not*, still suffers such anguish over its national identity. For the 26 million Canadians, what seems remarkable is that anyone would comment on this, so ingrained and natural does such perpetual pondering seem.

Canadian?

Americans have long been ignorant about most aspects of Canada, but at least they see it as one country. Canadians, instead, have mostly seen their land as a large variety of pieces always separated by wide gaps and until recently not often visited by each other.

To define what an American is, schoolchildren in the United States might lapse into the past, recalling names like Abigail Adams, George

Washington, Abraham Lincoln, Frederick Douglass, and others from the country's colorful history. They can talk about the Revolutionary War or the Civil War or Pearl Harbor, the great flood of immigrants at various times, and the civil rights movement. And an American child could talk about these things regardless of where he or she grew up. Americans, it seems, assume they know who they are. And that assumption is largely shared across the continent.

Not in Canada, which has had no Revolution, no Civil War, no broad mythology of national heroes for all to share. The first prime minister of Canada, for instance, is not revered as a national father through fables about how he could never tell a lie. He was Sir John A. Macdonald, a dour Scot, a tough politician, and an alcoholic whose name is often misspelled and whose birthday (January 11, 1815) is not only not a holiday—it is largely unknown.

Canadians do, however, religiously celebrate the May birthday of Queen Victoria, the British sovereign whose day now passes unnoticed in her own homeland. She was queen when Canada was created by Britain in 1867. Possibly the only "hero" of national stature most Canadians know is Louis Riel, a half-Indian whose western rebellions in the late 1800's symbolized the bitter French-English linguistic divisions that still trouble Canada at times.

Canada was created as a country not by Canadians demanding control of their own land but, hastily, by a British Parliament that, in 1867, was worried that an aggressive, expansive United States might send its idle armies north again, as it had during the War of 1812. (To this day, American pupils learn about the British burning of Washington, D.C., in that conflict but not that it came in retaliation for the sacking of Toronto by U.S. troops.)

At the time of Canada's creation in 1867, the United States had the largest military forces in the world. The Civil War was recently over and Britain's support for the Confederacy was still fresh in the minds of

A Canadian Rebel

In 1869 Louis Riel (pronounced ree-EL) led a rebellion of *métis* (people born to European, mainly French, trappers and Indian women) in the area that would become Manitoba, north of Minnesota and North Dakota. When the Canadian government bought considerable land from the Hudson's Bay Company, Riel's followers feared they would lose their land to new settlers.

When nonviolent protests failed, Riel and his followers seized Fort Garry, which was to become Winnipeg, Manitoba's capital. Government forces put down the rebellion the next year. Riel, classified an outlaw, fled. But in creating the province of Manitoba, the government did set aside land for the *métis*. In 1873 and 1874 Riel was elected to Canada's House of Commons, but never took his seat. In 1875 the government granted the rebel leader a pardon on the condition that he leave the country.

But Riel had a nervous breakdown and spent the next few years in insane asylums. He then emigrated to Montana and became a U.S. citizen. By 1884, many of his followers had moved west themselves, into what became Saskatchewan, where the arrival of new settlers from the East reignited their fears of displacement. A delegation went to Montana and pleaded for his return. In the winter of 1885 Riel did just that. He proclaimed a provisional *métis* government. Fighting erupted against government troops, who crushed the rebellion. After surrendering, Riel was convicted of treason and hanged.

His death ended the rebellions. But it also put another lasting scar on the relations between English- and French-speaking Canadians.

many Americans, who announced the end of a reciprocal trade treaty with Canada. In addition, the government in Washington had just leapfrogged western Canada to buy Alaska from Russia for $7.2 million. Known in Washington as "Seward's Folly" after Secretary of State William H. Seward, who proposed it, the sale was seen as a waste of money. But in London, where Canadian territory was seen as a safe land route to the Orient and India, the purchase was very threatening. The vast lands of colonial Canada had to be made safe.

Six Hours Due North

But vast is too small a word for Canada. It is the second-largest country in the world, a distorted parallelogram of almost 4 million square miles (10 million square kilometers) of land and inland waters stretching far beyond the imagination of traditionally insular Canadians. East to west, Canada spans 4,545 miles (7,313 kilometers) and six of the world's twenty-four time zones. South to north, Canada stretches almost 3,000 miles (5,000 kilometers), farther than New York City to Los Angeles. Airplanes take off from southern Canada and fly due north for six hours before landing. Even then, they are still hundreds of miles from the end of Canadian territory near the top of the world.

The smallest of Canada's ten provinces, Prince Edward Island, is still almost twice as large as the smallest American state, Rhode Island. The single province of Quebec stretches as far as from New York City to Omaha. Four Great Britains could fit inside British Columbia and nearly three Frances inside just Quebec. Three Japans could fit inside the boundaries of Ontario, which has fewer residents than the city of Tokyo.

And Canada's two northern territories—the Northwest Territories and the Yukon—are alone larger in area than West Germany, France, Britain, Italy, Egypt, Austria, Spain, Portugal, and all the New England

and Middle Atlantic states put together. Yet these two territories, sprawling, frozen landscapes that cover more than 40 percent of Canada and are home to fewer people than attend most professional football games, are not yet fully incorporated into Canada as provinces.

And overlying the physical geography is a mental mountain range of divisions, most prominently the very real threat that someday the French-speaking province of Quebec will break away into some form of independence, physically dividing Canada and destroying its historic self-image as a tolerant and peaceful haven of bilingualism.

Adrift on this country's overwhelming landscape are 26 million people, three quarters of them huddled along the boundary with the United States. The rest of the country is left to hardy pioneers, still homesteading or battling the sea as the twentieth century draws to a close, and to all kinds of ordinary and exotic wildlife from muskrats to polar bears. In the Yukon one caribou herd is so large it can take a full day for all the animals to pass just one rock. The country is so big and still so empty—Canada has less population density, for instance, than even Saudi Arabia—that the federal government spends more than $150 million a year just investigating reports of people lost or in trouble in planes and boats.

Canadians are so subdivided by the distance and size of their land, by the physical barriers of mountain ranges and endless bogs that dominate it, and by varying traditions and even languages that there has been very little sense among Canadians of their geographic whole. "The fundamental question in English Canada," said Northrop Frye, the late Canadian scholar, "is not, 'Who am I?' but 'Where is here?' "*

Cities

Presiding over this array of allegiances is Ottawa, a cold, old canal town chosen as the country's compromise capital by Queen Victoria, who

*Northrop Frye, "Thoughts of a Great Scholar," *Maclean's* (April 5, 1982), p. 43.

never saw Canada. Nearby is Montreal, once the premier city in North America. Montreal remains the commercial capital of Canada's French-speaking populace. But thanks to economic and political-linguistic forces beyond its control, it has, like Boston in the United States, seen its powerful national importance dwindle to only regional prominence. Quebec City, where British troops defeated the French in 1759 to unite Canada under one colonial power, remains the political capital of French-speaking Canada and a scenic pocket of Old World architecture on the cliffs overlooking the once-formidable rapids in the St. Lawrence River.

Once, a single city dominated the entire land. Now there are several, each specializing in some economic areas, each rapidly growing in prominence, and, as always in Canada, each quick to protect jealously its newfound strengths. There is Halifax, once the starting point for World War II convoys ferrying supplies to besieged Britain, now a commercial hub and harbor home to deep-sea oil-drilling rigs. There is St. John's, still a tiny port on a stormy North Atlantic and now the capital of Canada's newest province, Newfoundland, which remained a piece of Britain's colonial empire until 1949. There is Winnipeg, the St. Louis of Canada, pragmatic prairie capital of Manitoba, home to agricultural commodities traders and producer of aggressive, imaginative business executives. There is Calgary, Canada's Houston, a bustling boom town of modern skyscrapers fueled by oil and humanity's search for it and, in 1988, an international window into Canada as energetic host to the winter Olympics. And there is Vancouver, a developing financial capital for the burgeoning Pacific-rim countries that is tucked between snowcapped mountains and the broad, blue Pacific, with a moderate climate that resembles northern California's.

The clock on the Parliament Building in Ottawa shows that it is already dark at 5:05 P.M. Government of Canada, ISTC

The Ontario Octopus   Still presiding over this scattered scene, though increasingly wary of its wily challengers for national power, sits Toronto, the old Indian winter camp whose once-muddy lanes are lined

Toronto's Eaton Centre is part of the largest underground shopping complex in North America, though this section is aboveground.   Metro Toronto Convention & Visitors Association

now with sprawling underground malls and eye-catching steel and glass buildings housing many of the huge corporations that control Canada's economy. A 244-square-mile (632-square-kilometer) metropolis once called York, Toronto remains home to nearly one out of every eight Canadians and is still the preeminent center of Canadian business, finance, culture, fashion, publishing, and communications. The unofficial capital of English-speaking Canada, Toronto remains the symbol for most Canadians of the "Ontario Octopus," that hated complex of power networks that has for so long seemed to control all of Canada's geographic regions for the long-term benefit of only one, itself at the center.

Some countries are united by geography. A major river, for instance, unites the people along its banks with the same irrigation, food supplies, and transportation highway. But Canada is divided by its geography, as Canada's political leaders discovered long ago whenever they tried to fashion a single national policy on any issue from oil to even the wording of the national anthem, "O Canada." These varied, sprawling, separate provincial kingdoms have few things in common with each other save their dogged determination to remain separate, their abiding suspicion of each other, and, oftentimes, their natural and economic attraction to an adjacent American region that is greater than their links to any distant section of Canada. In Canada, even the rivers add to divisions; they flow the wrong way—toward the north, where nobody is.

Novelist Hugh MacLennan has written eloquently of Canada's two solitudes—the English and the French—simultaneously living together in the same land yet apart in language, culture, spirit, and perhaps someday, in political structure. In reality, however, it is Canada's harsh geography that has made it less a homogeneous nation with a common identity and more of a collection of regional solitudes separated by formidable natural barriers and from their natural American neighbors by artificial political boundaries.

One Country, Two Anthems

Canada is one country. But to satisfy the feelings of its two largest language groups—the English and French—the government deemed it necessary to have three sets of lyrics for the land's single national anthem, "O Canada"—one in English, one in French, and another compromise version that mixes both English and French.

Here are the three versions, first the English, then the English translation of the French, and then the bilingual version:

English:

O Canada! Our home and native land,
True patriot love in all thy sons command.
With glowing hearts we see thee rise,
The true north strong and free!
From far and wide, O Canada,
We stand on guard for thee.
God keep our land glorious and free!

French:

O Canada, land of our ancestors,
Your head is crowned with glorious ornaments!
Because your arm knows how to handle a sword,
It can carry a cross.
Your history is an epic of the most brilliant achievements,
And your courage, dipped in faith,
Will protect our homes and our rights.

Bilingual:

O Canada! our home notre pays
La feuille d'érable: One flag from sea to sea.
Sol de liberté, sol d'égalite, Where freedom's banner flies;
Chantons tous la gloire d'une riche histoire,
Our home 'neath northern skies.
O Canada! O ma patrie! Hold high the Maple leaf o'er land and sea;
O Canada, my country, mon pays.

The Land

Spanning half the country in a semisterile swath, splattered across Quebec, northern Ontario, Manitoba, and Saskatchewan and on into the Northwest Territories, lies the Canadian Shield. It is a 700-million-year-old mass of elemental bedrock that serves as Canada's geological foundation, its most prominent feature, and a stark reminder to Canadians of their geography's brooding presence. As E. J. Pratt, a Canadian poet, once described the Shield, it is "too old for death, too old for life."

The Land of Cain

For many hundreds of thousands of years two massive ice sheets several miles thick pressed and scraped their way across much of what was to

Canadian Geographical Highlights

Largest Province	Quebec	594,858 square miles (1,540,681 square kilometers)
Largest City (area)	Gagnon, Que.	2,185 sq. mi. (5,660 sq. km.)
Largest Metropolitan Area (pop.)	Toronto, Ont.	3,427,200*
Largest Island	Baffin, NWT	195,927 sq. mi. (507,451 sq. km.)
Longest River	Mackenzie, NWT	2,636 mi. (4,241 km.)
Highest Mountain	Mt. Logan, Yukon	19,638 feet (5,951 meters)
Largest Lake (entirely in Canada)	Great Bear, NWT	12,096 sq. mi. (31,328 sq. km.)
Largest Lake (partly in Canada)	Superior	11,590 sq. mi. (29,888 sq. km.) in Canada; 20,986 sq. mi. (54,355 sq. km.) in U.S.A.
Deepest Lake	Great Slave, NWT	2,026 feet (614 meters)

*Based on 1986 census estimate.

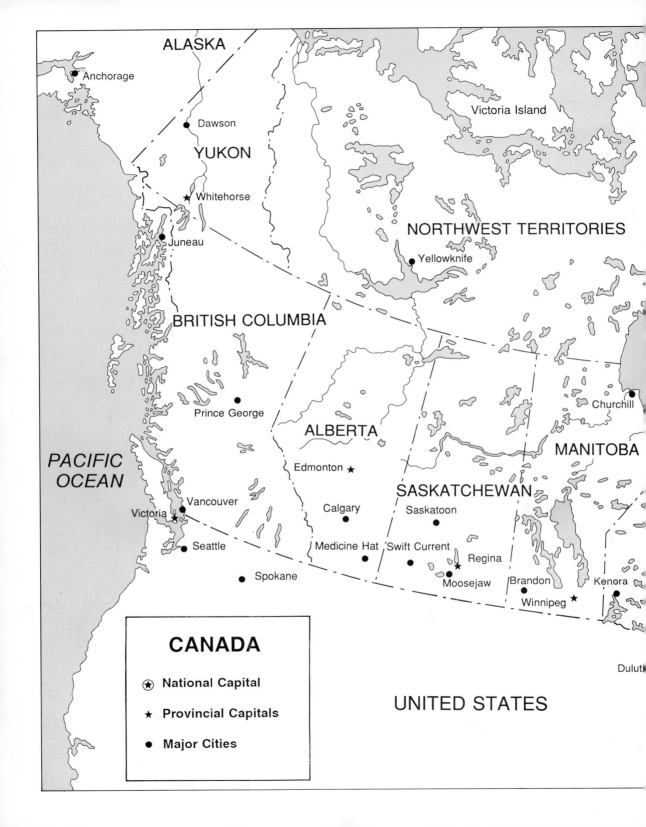

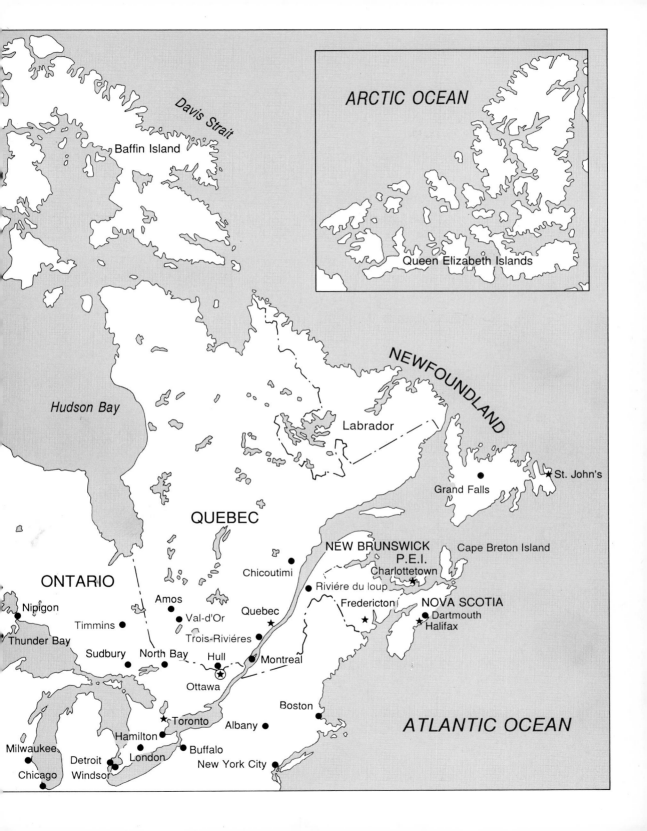

become Canada, crushing an entire mountain range before withdrawing to the north in a glacial retreat that lasted 6,000 years. These marauding ice fields left behind only sparse pockets of arable soil, thousands of lakes, muskeg bogs, and bug-laden swamps that constitute, in effect, a 1,000-mile-wide (1,600-kilometer-wide) corridor of inhospitable wilderness severing Canada's east from its west. It was the rock-strewn specter of this Shield that prompted Jacques Cartier, the French explorer, to note in his diary in 1534: "I am rather inclined to believe that this is the land God gave to Cain." This wilderness expanse was free of any through highway until 1943. And even more than forty years after that, long parts of Canada's single transcontinental road remained rugged and two-laned though mercifully free of tolls.

The Atlantic Provinces

Canada is divided into numerous major regions. In the east are the Maritime and Atlantic provinces—Nova Scotia, New Brunswick, Prince Edward Island, and Newfoundland.* They rarely seem to fit into Canada. The first three were concerned over the country's formation in 1867 because it meant severing important economic, transportation, emotional, and family ties to New England, which is still sometimes called "the Boston states" by Canadians. Years later, many decades before Quebec garnered global attention for its efforts to seek separation, Nova Scotia's legislature passed a resolution to secede from Canada.

Together, the four Atlantic provinces are about six times the size of

*Though often confused, even by Canadians, the Maritime and Atlantic provinces are not identical. The first three provinces alone make up the Maritimes; together with Newfoundland they form the Atlantic provinces.

Maine in area. They comprise 40 percent of the country's provinces, 6 percent of the area, and 10 percent of the country's population. They do, however, contain a larger share of the country's problems. Rural, rustic, rolling, and proud, these provinces have withered at Canada's back door as a chronic center of high unemployment.

Like Appalachia in the United States, Canada's Maritimes are beautiful to look at—largely unspoiled green hills of trees, rocks, berry patches, and vast bogs laced with tiny, tidy communities—but very hard to make a modern living in. Rough-hewn areas steeped in their own traditions, they have economies based on natural resources and a few factories transplanted by government incentives. But these are usually distant from major cities and must struggle to survive in a modern, technological era built on selling to mass markets.

Government Aid

Canadians have been very generous to each other in their governmental efforts to balance the economic inequities of life across their vast land.

Every year the federal government, now under increasing pressures to trim its budget spending, makes billions of dollars in payments to the poorer provinces, such as those on Canada's Atlantic coast, in an attempt to fund the kind of local government and lifestyle that more prosperous Canadians take for granted elsewhere. In some years, according to official estimates, government spending of all kinds accounts for more than 80 percent of all the economic activity in the poorer Atlantic provinces.

Additionally, federal and local governments have spent many billions of dollars in tax breaks, incentives, subsidies, and sometimes outright cash payments to encourage companies to open and maintain factories, mines, mills, and other operations, even where the immediate local

Provincial and Territorial Populations

Canada Total   26,584,064 (1990)

Ontario	9,373,000	Nova Scotia	881,000
Quebec	6,619,000	New Brunswick	712,000
British Columbia	2,961,000	Newfoundland	567,000
Alberta	2,385,000	Prince Edward Island	128,000
Manitoba	1,082,000	Northwest Territories	52,000
Saskatchewan	1,011,000	Yukon	25,000

(Source: Census of Canada, based on Jan. 1, 1988 estimates)

market could not support such a facility. One massive petroleum refinery was constructed on an isolated bay called Come-by-Chance in Newfoundland. It now sits, empty and abandoned. An expensive steel mill on scenic Cape Breton in Nova Scotia caused some grumbling when taxpayers elsewhere learned how many millions in federal subsidies were pouring in there every year to keep several hundred jobs alive.

Attracted by long-term tax breaks, cash payments, and welcoming provincial legislation designed to cripple union-organizing efforts, at least one foreign company, Michelin, the French tire maker, invested heavily in Nova Scotia factories. And some smaller-scale homegrown "industry" did succeed with a little imagination.

Peggy's Cove Lighthouse in Nova Scotia.   Government of Canada, ISTC

New Brunswick

Capital	Fredericton
Population	712,000
Total Area	28,355 sq. mi. (73,440 sq. km.)
Land Area	27,834 sq. mi. (72,090 sq. km.)
Length of Coastline	947 mi. (1,524 km.)
Major Industries	Fishing, manufacturing, mining, forestry, pulp and paper
Minerals Produced	Zinc, silver, lead, coal, copper, and stone
Number of Farms	2,776

Newfoundland

Capital	St. John's
Population	567,000
Total Area	156,649 sq. mi. (405,720 sq. km.)
Land Area	143,510 sq. mi. (371,690 sq. km.)
Length of Coastline	12,256 mi. (19,720 km.)
Major Industries	Fishing, pulp and paper, hydroelectric production, mining, and manufacturing
Minerals Produced	Iron, asbestos, zinc, sand, and gravel
Number of Farms	415

Nova Scotia

Capital	Halifax
Population	881,000
Total Area	21,425 sq. mi. (55,490 sq. km.)
Land Area	20,402 sq. mi. (52,840 sq. km.)
Length of Coastline	3,688 mi. (5,934 km.)
Major Industries	Fishing, manufacturing, mining, tourism, forestry, and agriculture
Minerals Produced	Coal, gypsum, sand, and gravel
Number of Farms	3,170

Prince Edward Island

Capital	Charlottetown
Population	128,000
Total Area	2,185 sq. mi. (5,660 sq. km.)
Land Area	2,185 sq. mi. (5,660 sq. km.)
Length of Coastline	688 mi. (1,107 km.)
Major Industries	Tourism, fishing, agriculture, and light manufacturing
Minerals Produced	Sand and gravel
Number of Farms	2,458

Newfoundland

Newfoundland, first found by John Cabot in 1497, just five years after Columbus stumbled onto the Caribbean, remains apart from Canada with the country's highest unemployment rate and smallest per-person income. It is a Tennessee-size island slightly closer to Liverpool, England, than to Toronto. Everything there is shaped by the uncertainties that accompany a life still controlled by such powerful natural forces as the Arctic and the sea. With its own English dialect, frequent insulating fogs, its own diverse island traditions, and even its own time zone, 30 minutes off everyone else's hour, Newfoundland is connected to the mainland by airplanes that are often crippled by the weather, by television and radio signals bounced off space satellites, and by storm-tossed ferries that must also be icebreakers to dodge the icebergs like the one that sank the *Titanic* nearby. On that rugged island province there is an intriguing local expression: "Nofty was forty when he lost the pork." It is not translatable literally, but it refers to the score of a Newfoundland card game that suddenly turns against the leading scorer. It is often said as a homespun warning that the uncertainties of a brief life and a harsh land must always be kept in mind to temper any sudden hopes for anything better.

Newfoundland was Great Britain's first overseas colony. Originally it was just an offshore fishing platform for European fleets, which arrived with the good weather and left in the fall, their holds full of cod, haddock, and the area's other abundant sea life. To this day, Canada remains the world's largest fish-exporting country. But the combination of modern methods and foreign fleets is producing serious overfishing. In the beginning the forests produced the tall, sturdy woods that the Royal Navy prized so highly to uphold the sails of its distant ships. The Atlantic region had bounteous supplies of underground—and under-

Caribou in the Torngat Mountains, Labrador, Newfoundland. Native Canadians hunt caribou and use every part of the animal down to the sinew, which is used as sewing thread.
Rod Beebe/SportsLight

sea—coal. But as Canada entered the age of industry and steamships, the Atlantic region's coal was shipped elsewhere for use; now much of it must find markets overseas, which is good for Canada's economy but does little to spawn new jobs locally. Canadian industry did not come eagerly to the east, there being no large-scale local markets, and the larger ones that did exist in Canada were so distant. Even goods arriving from overseas tended to bypass the Atlantic ports and costly transfer to railroads there in favor of a single faster, less expensive journey by water up the St. Lawrence River. Later, they could go even farther up,

Living off Christmas Trees

"For us," said Pat Septon, "we make it when we can." Mr. Septon works in eastern Canada's Christmas-tree industry. All over Nova Scotia, Quebec, and New Brunswick, the brattling sounds of chain saws echo through the woods from the middle of October until early December.

Their harvest is mostly ten- to twelve-year-old balsam trees, which are bundled, six or eight to a bale, and trucked around the clock to sales lots often more than 2,000 miles away. Sometimes one truck will load in Nova Scotia on Monday, deliver 1,600 trees to Milwaukee, and be home again by Friday. At times six-truck convoys will drive the entire North American east coast to deliver nearly 10,000 trees to a freighter waiting in Miami and bound for South America, where Christmas comes in their summertime.

Such intense seasonal, or cyclical, work tied to demand among distant consumers is typical of many local Canadian economies. Now, they are increasingly sophisticated. There was a time when fallers simply walked through the woods and cut down any tree.

along the St. Lawrence Seaway, which could carry cargoes to the north shore of Lake Superior, almost all the way to the prairies.

And like Canada's western provinces, the eastern ones often could have purchased cheaper American-made products from nearby United States markets. But due to legislation and tariffs designed to protect homegrown Canadian industry, most of it concentrated in the more populous, and thus more politically powerful, provinces of Ontario and Quebec, eastern and western Canadians were forced to buy Canadian products, often at higher prices.

Now the trees and their land are carefully managed year-round.

One tree farm near Halifax in Nova Scotia, the largest tree-exporting province, spans 30,000 acres, nearly 47 square miles (12,000 hectares, or 121 square kilometers). As those woodlands are cleared of larger trees for timber and pulp, Christmas trees are planted behind. Beginning at age three or four, the trees are individually cultivated and fertilized according to the needs of that particular soil and tree crop for fast, full growth. They are annually trimmed to stimulate new buds and the bushy shape that Canadian growers know foreign buyers prize. These trees are ready for harvest in one quarter the time it takes a good timber tree to mature in that climate.

By December 9 every year, just as city buyers are beginning to buy their holiday tree, all of Mr. Septon's quarter million trees will have been shipped south. Typically, a tired Mr. Septon has forgotten to cut one for his own family. "But you know," he said, "after handling all those trees for all these years, I'm not too fussy about having one of my own."

Answering Ads from 1,000 Miles Away

While the Atlantic provinces have produced four prime ministers and still do turn out pockets of success in local agricultural areas, significant numbers of conscientious laborers remain unemployed or have had to move elsewhere; central Canadian factories quickly learned that an excellent channel to eager workers is the "Help Wanted" ad columns of newspapers more than 1,000 miles away in cities such as St. John's, Newfoundland.

Recurring disappointments and false hopes of gold someday lining the streets of their tidy, scenic communities fed a kind of inspiring regional pride and a pessimism that echoed in the national mind as well. According to one skit by the Royal Canadian Air Farce (correct), a homegrown comedy troupe, "Some people look at things as they are and say, 'Why?' A Canadian looks at things as they might be and says, 'No way!'"

A harbor in St. John's, the capital of Newfoundland, Canada's newest province and Britain's first overseas territory.   Government of Canada, ISTC

Quebec

To the west of the Maritimes and just up the wide St. Lawrence River, which is frozen shut one third of every year, is Quebec, the largest province. There, clustered along the broad, rocky river-bottom land and around the weathered spires of each little community's Roman Catholic church, is where settlement of Canada by Europeans actually began on farm fields designed to be narrow to maximize the number of families with riverfront access. It is also home for most of the country's French-speaking Canadians, one quarter of the country's population, and for the province's two principal cities—Quebec and Montreal. It is no accident that they are where they are; they are both on a river (the St. Lawrence) because that was the best way to travel in the early days and the river at both cities was narrow and full of rapids. So the ships had to stop.

And nearby, upstate New York's system of lakes and rivers also provided a convenient doorway for Montreal's aggressive commercial interests into the American colonies. The British army and its Indian allies and American revolutionaries later used the same waters as handy invasion routes against each other.

Ontario

To the north of Montreal and Quebec, almost immediately upon leaving both cities, is again the imposing wilderness and sometimes beauty of the Shield. There, the roads are few or nonexistent and the country remains untamed by the concrete and straight lines of human civilization. The same country flows farther west into the empty woods and leaky mines of northern Ontario, where lonely railroad trains slowly winding through forests bent low beneath the weight of heavy snows

Gaspé Peninsula, Quebec.   Canadian Government Office of Tourism

still stop along the way for trappers and anyone else who flags them down from trackside. Southern Ontario dips down into the American heartland atop the Great Lakes so far south that travelers from Windsor, Ontario, must go back north to get to Detroit. Southern Ontario is another world of tidy, lush green farms neatly linked to scores of industrial communities, some not so tidy, that produce fully half of Canada's manufacturing output.

Quebec

Capital	Quebec City
Population	6,619,000
Total Area	594,857 sq. mi. (1,540,680 sq. km.)
Land Area	523,857 sq. mi. (1,356,790 sq. km.)
Length of Coastline	6,736 mi. (10,839 km.)
Major Industries	Manufacturing, agriculture, mining, meat processing, petroleum refining, and hydroelectricity generation
Minerals Produced	Gold, asbestos, copper, zinc, stone, and iron ore
Number of Farms	37,160

Ontario

Capital	Toronto
Population	9,373,000
Total Area	412,579 sq. mi. (1,068,580 sq. km.)
Land Area	344,088 sq. mi. (891,190 sq. km.)
Length of Coastline	752 mi. (1,210 km.)
Major Industries	Manufacturing, finance, tourism, construction, agriculture, and forestry
Minerals Produced	Nickel, gold, copper, uranium, zinc, sand and gravel, and stone
Number of Farms	63,253

This skating rink is part of the lakefront development in Toronto. An industrial shoreline has been transformed into a recreation area for popular use.   Rod Beebe/SportsLight

Manitoba and Saskatchewan

To the west, beginning at the distinct Ontario border, the Canadian prairies emerge, flat, fairly fertile, and ferociously uncompromising. These broad, semiarid plains atop the American Dakotas span the two provinces of Manitoba (a combination of Sioux and Assiniboine words meaning "prairie water") and Saskatchewan (a corruption of the Cree word *kisiskatchewan* or "swift-flowing"). There, grains and trains dominate life. The grains use the strong sun but aren't usually hurt by the absence of abundant moisture. Trains are still vital because Canada is not blessed with the same massive inland river system whose watery veins drain the water, crops, and goods of the interior United States. Bulky wheat, rye, barley, and oilseeds must be moved by Canada's overstressed and underfinanced rail system, the privately owned Canadian Pacific Railroad and the government-owned Canadian National system.

Being so open to the unpredictable, uncontrollable elements can be a harsh life and one that tempers any optimism. As recently as the 1920's and 1930's, the so-called "dirty thirties," locusts and drought consumed crops, sawdust sold for more than wheat, and a child's daily chores before school could include breaking the morning ice on the washbasin. Saturday could mean a trip to town in a large sled drawn by a horse and heated by bricks taken from the stove and placed on the floorboards.

An aerial view of the prairie near Marquette, Manitoba. The grain elevators hold crops near railroad sidings. They will be sold overseas by a federal government agency.
Canadian Government Office of Tourism

The North   In the north of both provinces, far beyond the reach of year-round roads and telephone lines, and spilling over to the west into neighboring Alberta, runs the Shield again like some geographical theme uniting Canadians in adversity. Some of the communities here remain essentially frontier forts, resupply points for trappers and natives where furs are still traded for knives, flour, and shirts. Some of these communities are disposable towns, there to mine some mineral from the ground while the price is right in the United States, Germany, or Japan, and then to disappear. Others are mere government outposts, where residents get isolation pay and wily wolves eat unwary pets. In this countryside, frozen rivers become local roadways many months of the year. Airplanes are the only reliable link to "the outside." And trackless trains of bulldozers dragging huge skidding sleds of fuels and foods to distant settlements crunch their way through the long winters, the vast woods, and the frozen swamps at four or five miles per hour.

p65

Manitoba

Capital	Winnipeg
Population	1,082,000
Total Area	250,946 sq. mi. (649,950 sq. km.)
Land Area	211,722 sq. mi. (548,360 sq. km.)
Length of Coastline	563 mi. (917 km.)
Major Industries	Agriculture, slaughtering and meat processing, manufacturing, and mining
Minerals Produced	Nickel, copper, oil, zinc, and gold
Number of Farms	25,262

Saskatchewan

Capital	Regina
Population	1,011,000
Total Area	251,865 sq. mi. (652,330 sq. km.)
Land Area	220,347 sq. mi. (570,700 sq. km.)
Major Industries	Agriculture, mining, meat processing, petroleum refining, and hydroelectricity generation
Minerals Produced	Oil, uranium, natural gas, coal, and sulphur
Number of Farms	60,809

Alberta

Alberta (named for a daughter of Queen Victoria) has seen rapid change in recent times. From its rugged northern wilderness, where bushy buffalo still roam freely, to its southern rolling rangelands along the Montana boundary, Alberta once was a dusty, rural backwater specializing in cattle, grains, and breathtaking Rocky Mountain scenery. But in 1947 Albertans began finding vast quantities of oil and gas beneath the province. Eventually, this resource lead to furious economic growth in many sectors of the province, establishing Edmonton, the political capital, and Calgary, the oil capital, as major cities within Canada. In Calgary's case, it also led to hosting the 1988 Winter Olympics and a brief spot on the world's televised stage.

The skyline of Calgary, Alberta, with the Saddledome in the foreground.   Government of Canada, ISTC

Alberta

Capital	Edmonton
Population	2,385,000
Total Area	255,286 sq. mi. (661,190 sq. km.)
Land Area	298,799 sq. mi. (644,390 sq. km.)
Major Industries	Oil production, mining, agriculture and beef ranching, manufacturing, and construction
Minerals Produced	Oil, natural gas, sulphur, and coal
Number of Farms	51,743

Oil

Ironically, in a quintessentially Canadian way, Alberta's underground riches with their accompanying growth and prosperity did not become bonds of good fortune and affluence for present and future generations of Canadians. Instead, through jealousy and fear they became genuine threats to the fragile foundations of national unity, pitting one geographic region against another.

While the United States imported nearly half of its massive daily petroleum supplies, Alberta's oil gave Canada 80 percent energy self-sufficiency. Canadians for a long while enjoyed petroleum prices less than half that of the rest of the world. And the rate they burned up their energy, combined with their severe climate and grand distances, made Canada the greatest per-person consumer of energy in the industrialized world.

But under Canada's loose federal system, the provinces control much more than, for instance, individual American states do. In Canada, provinces control their own onshore resources but are required to meet certain federal pricing policies. This means there are tension-filled regular negotiations between federal and provincial governments over the price that the rest of the country will pay for Alberta's petroleum supplies. This has pitted Albertans, whose petroleum revenues enabled them not to have sales taxes and still have gasoline at two thirds the price of other provinces, against the energy-consuming regions, which enjoyed a bargain by any other country's standards. But this power and prosperity also fueled a feeling of self-confidence in western Canada, although it did not change the political representation in Canada's House of Commons, where Ontario and Quebec still held the balance of power with more members than their populations warranted.

British Columbia

The remaining link in the resource-rich west is British Columbia, a self-contained economic empire that is 1.3 times larger than Texas. It is cut off from the rest of Canada by mountains, a moderate coastal climate, its own time zone (shared with the Yukon), and an air of genial superiority. It was the first Canadian region to consider independence. But in the late nineteenth century, Britain retained considerable influence in Canada, which is still a member of the British Commonwealth. And so in 1871 British Columbia was promised a rail link to the east with the building of a transcontinental railroad as a condition of its entering the Confederation.

Those rails are one of the few national bonds for British Columbia, inevitably referred to as B.C. It is a beautiful area where landslides, snows, and rampaging rivers can cut off rail access from the rest of the country for days. The province is still building roads and railroads to open its interior wilderness to development. Two thirds of the province is covered by trees, which are sawed and chipped and shipped to larger markets in the United States and Asia. The province also contains vast quantities of natural gas, coal, fish, orchards, and some oil, more than it could ever use itself. As one result, British Columbia has been less insular in its thinking than much of Canada. It has eagerly developed strong economic links with American states just up and down the coast and with the burgeoning markets of the developing countries scattered around the rim of the Pacific Ocean. Vancouver, which is 350 miles closer to Tokyo than it is to Halifax, is now the busiest port on the west coast of North America. And the city's gleaming skyscrapers, reflected on the bay's beautiful waters against a backdrop of snowcapped mountains, is the office home for scores of American companies. They employ one out of every five workers in the province. Vancouver is also popular

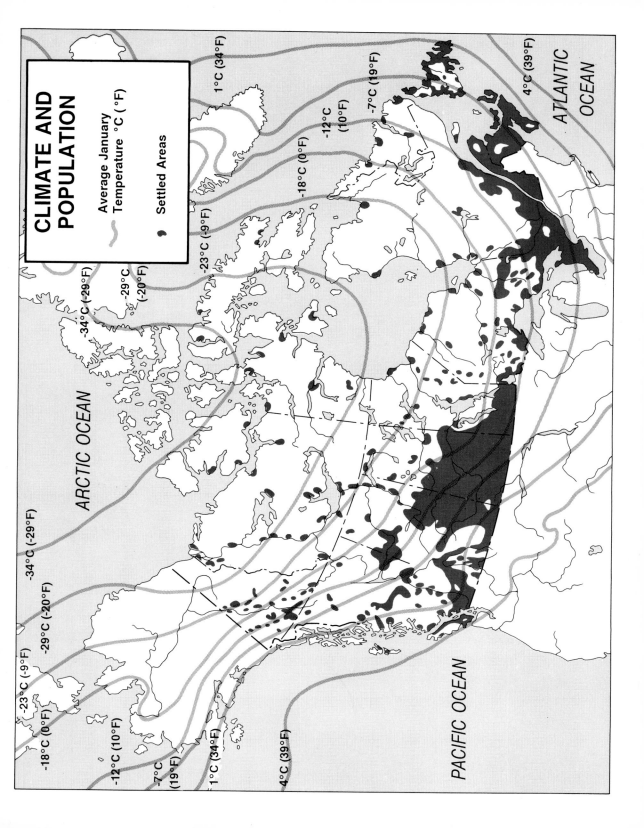

CLIMATE AND POPULATION

Average January
Temperature °C (°F)

Settled Areas

ARCTIC OCEAN

ATLANTIC OCEAN

PACIFIC OCEAN

4°C (39°F)

1°C (34°F)

-7°C (19°F)

-12°C (10°F)

-18°C (0°F)

-23°C (-9°F)

-29°C (-20°F)

-34°C (-29°F)

-34°C (-29°F)

-29°C (-20°F)

-23°C (-9°F)

-18°C (0°F)

-12°C (10°F)

-7°C (19°F)

1°C (34°F)

4°C (39°F)

Jutting into water, the ultramodern Vancouver Trade and Convention Centre was originally built as the Canada Pavilion at Expo '86.   Canadian Government Office of Tourism/ Allen Aerial Photos

among a growing number of international banks because its Pacific time zone enables them to simultaneously do business in Europe, on the east coast of North America, and in Asia.

Yukon

Shaped like a capital letter *L,* the Yukon (from *yucoo*, an Indian word meaning "clear water") sits atop British Columbia's internal wilderness, where authorities were so certain that it would somehow matter someday, they used chain saws to carve a 50-foot-wide, arrow-straight swath through empty woods to definitively mark the boundary between these two Canadian units. This territory contains enough space for five Pennsylvanias, twenty-one mountains more than two miles tall, fewer people (23,000) than a few city blocks in Toronto, and about 2,726 miles of road, only 119 of them paved. The pristine lakes there, where steamers and homemade rafts once hauled north excited gold seekers, most of them Americans, and then impoverished souls back south, lead to turbulent rivers that run past vast copper mines, abandoned sheds, and huge, long mounds of rocks that resemble the aftermath of a giant mole. They are, however, merely the natural refuse of nearly a century's frantic search for gold just outside fabled Dawson, where gold flakes in two average-looking creeks gave their names—"Klondike" and "Bonanza"—entirely new meanings. The same little community (average year-round population 350) also was home to a bank teller named Robert Service, the writer who gave English literature such memorable characters as Dangerous Dan McGrew and the perennially cold Sam McGee.

Today, while huge hoses steadily wash away nearby cliffs in the continuing hunt for gold, Dawson remains a muddy spot for tourists, most of them Americans, too. The local detachment of Mounties (the

British Columbia

Capital	Victoria
Population	2,961,000
Total Area	365,746 sq. mi. (947,800 sq. km.)
Land Area	358,969 sq. mi. (929,730 sq. km.)
Length of Coastline	11,098 mi. (17,856 km.)
Major Industries	Forestry, mining, tourism, fishing, agriculture, and manufacturing
Minerals Produced	Coal, copper, natural gas, oil, lead, zinc, and gold
Number of Farms	13,699

Yukon

Capital	Whitehorse
Population	25,000
Total Area	186,660 sq. mi. (483,450 sq. km.)
Land Area	184,931 sq. mi. (478,970 sq. km.)
Length of Coastline	213 mi. (343 km.)
Major Industries	Mining and tourism
Minerals Produced	Gold, silver, lead, zinc, and copper
Number of Farms	0

Royal Canadian Mounted Police is a combination federal law-enforcement arm like the F.B.I. and, in most provinces, also a state police) now includes women. And their duties include patrolling the 460-mile-long Dempster Highway, the two-lane dirt road that took twenty-two years to build and in 1980 became the first North American public road to cross the Arctic Circle. In the winter, daring truck convoys, carrying their own bulldozers and survival gear, may take two weeks to make the trip in twenty-four-hour darkness. In the summer, tourists with four-wheel drive vehicles—and many extra tires—can make it in two days and end up in the Northwest Territories.

Northwest Territories

Capital	Yellowknife
Population	52,000
Total Area	1,322,903 sq. mi. (3,426,320 sq. km.)
Land Area	1,271,436 sq. mi. (3,293,020 sq. km.)
Length of Coastline	69,142 mi. (111,249 km.)
Major Industries	Mining, oil and gas exploration and extraction, and trapping
Minerals Produced	Lead, zinc, oil, and natural gas
Number of Farms	0

Northwest Territories

The Northwest Territories (they are really only one, for now, despite the plural name) make up one third of Canada's land mass. It is actually a collection of isolated regions so large that residents of Inuvik in the western end traveling to Baffin Island on the eastern side need at least two days to fly there and end up one eighth of the way around the world. The regions of this vast territory vary from the flat scrubland in the west around Yellowknife, the territorial capital where trees can take several generations of very brief summers to grow as thick as a man's arm, to the groaning green ice of the Arctic Ocean, where schoolteachers pass leaves around their classrooms so Inuit children can touch what southern Canadians must rake. To the east are the treeless Scandinavian-type

The Alaska Highway begins at Dawson Creek, British Columbia, and ends at Fairbanks, Alaska. Paved in some sections, well-maintained gravel in others, it stretches for over 1,200 miles. Canadian Government Office of Tourism

The Arctic Circle crosses the end of Pangnirtung Fjord here on Baffin Island.   Andrew H. Malcolm

fjords of Baffin Island, where the frigid waters lead to the world's northernmost park, Auyuittuq (EYE-you-eetuck, or "place that never melts").

Britain did not relinquish its North American Arctic land holdings to Canada until several years after Canada's independence in 1867. Once little more than a frigid fur farm for the Hudson's Bay Company, one of the world's oldest continuing companies, and its competitors, Canada's far northern territories still constitute one third of the country's land area. Talks between the federal government and leaders of the native population have led to a tentative agreement to divide the Northwest Territories into two areas, one called Nunavit, which means "our land" in Inuktitut, the language of the Inuit, and the other called Denendeh, which means roughly the same in the language of the Dene Indians.

Ice

For 99.75 percent of Canada's population, ice is something to drop in a drink or sprinkle salt on in the driveway several months a year. But for the 63,000 other Canadians, ice is a brutal fact of life that unites them in hardship.

The frozen surface of the Arctic Ocean is one and a half times the size of the United States. It seems empty and barren. But it forms natural highways and bridges for wildlife to migrate and for humans to follow. So important is this frozen mass that in Inuktitut, the language of Canada's Inuit peoples, the giant polar ice cap that is always there dominating life is called "mother ice."

The ice covering some fjords is not so much a floor as it is a giant floating raft. It is used as a fishing platform, an oil-drilling platform, and a highway where heavily laden supply trucks (or dogsleds and snowmobiles) creep their way into wilderness areas that have never been cut by paved roads. The ice can be a racetrack for cars and snowmobiles. It supports scientific observation platforms that drift in the Arctic Ocean studying currents and deep-sea life. Cut in certain ways by skilled hands, ice can make a storm shelter or a homemade refrigerator to hold fresh-killed game frozen solid until spring. If no ice is handy, the catch can be covered with stones and water poured over it. The new ice preserves the meat and locks it in place against thieves, human or animal.

In movement, ice can also be an awesome sight. With hidden ocean currents beneath and strong winds above, the ice can change without warning from a smooth, snow-covered expanse offering safe passage, to a twisted, impassable jumble of pressure ridges and insurmountable mini-mountains. Ice floes can be divided by open lanes of freezing seawater or, worse yet, thin layers of white snow treacherously masking hidden cracks and saltwater slush that can swallow unsuspecting victims in seconds.

At times these huge plates of ice can even seem to talk. As they grind together, push up on top of each other, and struggle, crumble, and refreeze, these sheets of ice a mile or more across actually moan and groan, adding a haunting flavor to the Arctic void.

A polar bear in the Northwest Territories. These bears weigh over eight hundred pounds, can knock a seal's head off with a single swipe, can swim for miles, and migrate as far south as Churchill, Manitoba. Government of Canada, ISTC

Canadian Pride

The drive for such internal sovereignty by the native peoples is symbolic of a growing pride among many Canadians. In recent years the "Eskimos" launched a successful drive against using that word to define themselves, a move roughly similar to the desire among people once called Negroes to be called blacks or African-Americans. "Eskimo" literally means "eater of raw meat," a term given them by arriving Europeans such as Martin Frobisher, who also snatched a handful of Inuit to take back as living trinkets to a curious England. Even in the 1950's the Canadian government used numbers for its northern citizens instead of names. Then, as the 1990's began, the Canadian government, which also ran expensive education and health programs across the vast area, was negotiating to give the natives possession (though not the mineral rights) of thousands of square miles of land and hundreds of millions of dollars in land-settlement costs. This would break into pieces the territories drawn by white men and more realistically reflect the ethnic and cultural boundaries of the native bands, many of whom cannot communicate with each other because their dialects are so different.

Although these negotiations were initially ignored in more populous southern Canada, they were emotional issues because the move to divide further an already divided Canada came just as a growing number were beginning to shed the idea of Canada as a mere country and to feel more comfortable with the notion of Canada as a nation of diverse peoples with a common sense of purpose and identity.

CHAPTER III

Living on
the Land

Part of Canada's problem has been that it was not settled in successive waves of immigrants, first-, then second-, then third-generation Canadians moving inexorably across a fertile landscape and in so doing becoming with each day a generation more aware of their new land and their common interests. Instead, most of Canada's regions were settled directly from abroad. A family from, say, Scotland or Iceland would leave that country, cross the broad Atlantic on a steamship, and then take a train to a specific town where the Canadian immigration agent had placed them. Typically, they would join a growing cluster of similar families from the same homeland. And there, in the splendid isolation of northern Manitoba or wherever, they would speak the same language as they did in "the old country" and pass on the old-country customs

One of many ethnic festivals held in cities across Canada to celebrate the heritages of its diverse minorities. This Folklorama Festival is held in Winnipeg, Manitoba. Canadian Government Office of Tourism

to generation after generation with scant contact with their new North American neighbors.

"This pattern of settlement sharply differentiated the Canadian experience from the American," according to Cole Harris, a historian at the University of British Columbia. "[In the United States] the land was perceived as a garden as readily as a wilderness, and it attracted far more settlers and focussed European dreams. . . . The American occupation of an essentially welcoming land had the capacity to mold different peoples into a relatively homogeneous culture as it spread them over an astonishing area."* In Canada, said the historian, this merger was stymied by the harsh geography and climate.

Canada has grown up, then, not so much as a single country, stitched together by common cultures, language, and experiences, but as a collection of regions, physically and psychologically separate. This caused individual provinces to cling tenaciously to their political power, far more power than an individual American state. All this prompted Canadians to see themselves less as citizens of Canada than as citizens of Manitoba or Alberta or Ontario or Quebec or the Maritimes. And they all happened to be loosely grouped together as a country called Canada to protect themselves from the Americans. In its internal politics, for example, British Columbia is so self-contained and truly provincial that it has no west-coast equivalent of either of the two major national political parties, the Progressive Conservatives or the Liberals.

Hay-Sucking Farmers and Oil "Sheikhs"

Typically, Canadians will know something of their region and the adjacent American region and the highway south to the nearest winter sun

---

*Cole Harris, "The Emotional Structure of Canadian Regionalism," a lecture at McGill University, Montreal, March 17, 1981.

spot. But much of the rest of their own country has remained a very large blur imprisoned in negative stereotypes perpetuated by geography, indifference, ignorance, and a communications media that has lavished hour after hour and news column after news column on coverage of the United States, but only episodic glimpses of elsewhere in Canada. The popular mind thus has remained stuck in stereotypes—the stuffy, Calvinist Torontonians, French-speaking lumberjacks in plaid flannel shirts, drunken Indians, hay-sucking farmers, crazy Montreal taxi drivers, faddish British Columbians in hot tubs, meat-and-potatoes immigrants from Central Europe, and greedy Albertan "sheikhs," newly rich from oil. When Canadians tell ethnic jokes, they don't reach for another country; it's inevitably some other Canadian region, usually Newfoundland, that is the butt of the laughter.

Power and Place

Canada's economic geography generally reflects its political geography. Where conditions are harshest—within the inhospitable Shield, for instance, or farther north in the frozen Arctic—economic activity beyond simple sustenance is at a minimum. It is clustered in far-flung population pockets and largely based on local resources, both human and natural. Transportation into and out of such limited markets is costly and until recently often uneconomical, requiring many kinds of government subsidies. To this day many of Newfoundland's picturesque little fishing villages, the so-called outports, remain physically isolated with no roads going beyond the berry patches on the edge of town. In the 1950's and 1960's the provincial governments, under pressure from Ottawa, tried to save money by cutting off supply ferries and forcing the people to leave their old communities and congregate in larger, more efficient ones; the effort failed, as thousands refused to leave, despite their isolation, or sneaked back in. Eventually, the supply boats were resumed.

Conversely, where conditions are more geographically and climatically temperate—for example, farther south along the long border with the United States and its vast, hungry markets—attractive opportunities have been proportionately magnified. This makes for a larger, affluent population there, leaving the less fortunate mired in their problems elsewhere.

Disparity

Immense economic differences are thus physically built into Canada's regional city-states. The relative attractiveness of a place is controlled by the seasons, by world demand for a local product, or by one year's fluctuating commodity prices. Other shifts are timed more in terms of generations. For instance, the nineteenth-century prosperity of Canada's eastern provinces was beached, possibly permanently, when steel steamships came to dominate the seas, undercutting global demand for Maritime timber and tall masts. Today, as the supply of ore thins out beneath one northern town, founded simply to serve the mine, the mine shuts down—and so does the disposable community. It becomes, in effect, a modern-day ghost town in the bush, while its residents pack their belongings and their dreams, tear up their roots, and move on to the next mine site on barges by summer or, in winter, on hazardous ice highways across frozen lakes and rivers.

Conversely, as the demand for, and later, the ballooning price of, oil and gas fueled the wide-ranging hunt for more isolated basins of petroleum resources, the gritty image of hard-luck Alberta, down in the dust and dependent on cows, changed to that of a booming energy capital. Jobs, a highly prized resource in modern-day Canada, were plentiful, and officials laid plans for the next generation of prosperity.

Ruling the Regions   As a collection of separate regions, Canada is unusually ill equipped to cope with such extreme disparities. And

this has made governing such a place as a single nation a difficult challenge. In other varied lands such as the United States, for example, where there are 60 people per square mile, rising and falling supply and demand have played a significant balancing role in smoothing out economic inequalities. The natural demand for jobs in one place easily attracted job hunters from elsewhere. For instance, unemployed eastern factory workers had a wide selection of large, hospitable alternate cities to live and work in across 3,000 miles of developed nation. West Virginia miners needed to travel only a couple of hundred miles to the beckoning rubber plants of Akron, Ohio, or the tool-and-die shops of Cleveland. Laid-off auto workers could drive onto an expressway in suburban Detroit and, without encountering any obstacle more significant than a stoplight, carry their skills to a new employer in Houston's once-bustling energy industry.

But Canada, where there are only six people per square mile, has nowhere near the selection of cities or the scale of industries or jobs. A 200-mile move wouldn't even get a driver into the next province in a country where the distance across Ontario alone is the same as that between Dallas and Los Angeles. Because occupational skills have traditionally been tied so closely to the unique individual economies of a home region, fewer skills in Canada seem immediately portable; not many lobsters for a Nova Scotian to catch in Saskatchewan, not much prairie wheat to grow on Prince Edward Island, and not many factory jobs to be sought in New Brunswick—and there has been great reluctance to try.

Many Canadians did try to find work elsewhere. For them it was often like moving to a foreign land, leaving behind family and friendships, and living in a strange city where, for example, Newfoundlanders would congregate at a few stores and bars that featured their region's foods, music, drink, and gossip. As new technologies create new jobs that require new skills, some of these barriers are breaking down.

French-speaking residents of New Brunswick, Manitoba, or Quebec leaving their home province have no guarantee they will encounter anything French-speaking outside of an office of the officially bilingual federal government. English-speaking Canadians moving into Quebec, something that doesn't happen much anymore, have had no choice about the language of their children's school; it is French.

The refinery at a nickel mine in Thompson, Manitoba.   Rod Beebe/SportsLight

Defending Difference

Despite attempts at constitutionally protecting certain rights between provinces, there remain strong legal impediments to Canadians' mobility. Every province has a defensive network of legislation and regulations to make it difficult for newcomers. For instance, the Alberta Law Society, which controls that province's legal profession, has a rule forbidding its more than 3,300 resident members from practicing law in partnerships with attorneys from outside the province, effectively banning non-Alberta firms from opening branches in the province. If a Manitoba auto mechanic moves next door to Ontario, he cannot legally get a job in his trade for six months, thereby effectively limiting such moves to very rich auto mechanics. Newfoundland, which chronically has Canada's highest unemployment rate, keeps a registry of local workers, who must have hiring preference in the province's oil industry over anyone from any other province. Some of these impediments have eased in recent years as more Canadian companies became nationwide operations, necessitating transfer of employees back and forth and exposing them to Canada's many differences. Still, no one from outside tiny Prince Edward Island—and all but 110,000 Canadians are from outside Prince Edward Island—can buy waterfront property there. If a Quebec company bids to sell computers or buses in British Columbia, it will surely lose the competition unless the bid is more than 10 percent under the local company's. The Quebec government restricts bids on construction contracts to companies with headquarters in the work site's region.

Diminishing Differences   In part because of the inability of Canada to provide a balance of economic opportunities within the country, Canadians throughout their history have remained basically suspi-

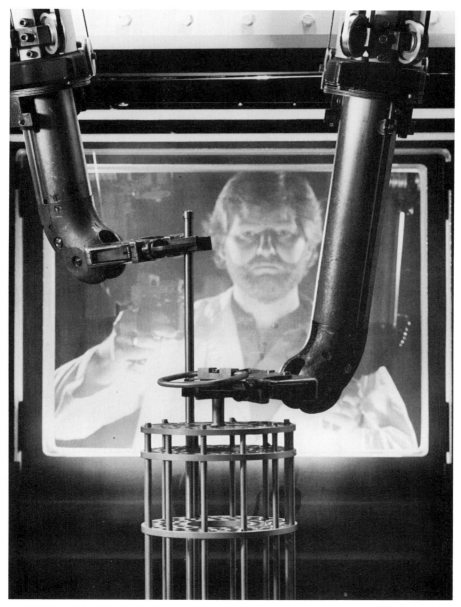

Lead glass protects a worker as he holds radioactive cobalt-60 with a remote arm and places it in a shipping cage at the Atomic Energy of Canada plant in Kanata, Ontario. Roger Ressmeyer/StarLight

cious of an open market, where independent buyers and sellers control price and profit. They have been basically receptive to deep government involvement and active intervention in many aspects of everyday life that would be labeled "interference" in some other societies, such as the United States.

Transfer Payments

From the beginning the government's goal has been to equalize life and opportunities. Through a complex—and costly—system of laws, traditions, regulations, policies, and fiscal formulas, Canada's federal government has also given mounting volumes of financial aid, called transfer payments, to the provinces. Whether for needs such as education, government health insurance plans, welfare support, subsidies to reduce fuel costs in isolated areas, or wilderness bonuses to attract qualified teachers and civil servants to distant domestic outposts, such assistance is designed to reinforce what is called "the social contract of Confederation." The goal is to smooth out the country's geographic and accompanying economic inequities and create in the process the crucial, unifying sense that all Canadians can gain from being participants in the same nation-building process regardless of where they happen to live.

Individual provinces do the same within themselves. They use spending by government-owned corporations, such as telephone and electric companies, to stimulate new economic growth or often simply to support the economy in troubled areas. Quebec, for instance, forced its own government pension plan to invest heavily in some private-resource companies, not to maximize earnings but to gain influence and control over company decisions affecting many workers and their communities. When the Quebec government wanted the provincial economy to grow faster, it had its giant utility, Quebec Hydro, launch new phases of a massive wilderness power project, and all that spending trickled down throughout the province; when the economy grew too hot and interest rates soared, the government told the utility to ease off the spending throttle.

One result, however, was a widely accepted, growing government role in the economy. In some years government spending in the broadest sense accounted for an estimated 86 percent of all economic activity in the poor Atlantic provinces. Even in Ontario, heart of Canada's manufacturing, the rate was 41 percent. Fully 20 percent of the federal budget was spent by simply being transferred to a provincial government. And, of course, the federal-provincial negotiations to set the size of these transfers provided yet another stage for rancorous talks among Canada's disparate provincial empires. In some provinces these transfer payments comprised half the governments' revenues.

Dependency

Such payments also create continuous pressures for new federal revenues—in other words, taxes. And they have aroused concern among many experts that these payments were creating a kind of creeping provincial welfare dependency. The transfer payments helped many individuals momentarily. The money likely stopped a further slide into poverty for others. And such official largesse allowed Canadians to feel good about their continuous battle against the difficulties of life and the challenges of their geography. But the payments also allowed the basic poverty cycle to continue and created a long-term economic and psychological dependency on governments of all kinds. These governments may not always have the money or the political will to continue such expensive economic Band-Aids. Indeed, as the 1980's ended, the Progressive Conservative government of Prime Minister Brian Mulroney moved to tighten eligibility rules on some benefits to save money and fight growing federal budget deficits.

Meanwhile, high unemployment—upward of 50 percent in some communities—continues with its accompanying family and social distress. Despite billions of dollars in help, economic growth in the Atlantic provinces stayed below the national average. The west enjoyed an energy boom ("It's the west's time in Confederation!" said one exhilarated provincial premier) and then stumbled into economic stagnation, while Quebec developed a vibrant economy—and considerable self-confidence—and Ontario in the middle enjoyed above-average economic growth, as it has throughout Canadian history. All this combined to widen the country's regional economic gaps.

The Landless Man

These gaps are a constant concern to Canada's fragile unity, especially during times of economic uncertainty when Canadian regions tend to fight among themselves more (good economic times let them grumble more about *perceived* injustices at the hands of the Americans). Canada, it was long said, is not so much a country as magnificent raw material for a country. Without painful but bonding wars, Canada has been, one prime minister observed, geographically impossible and politically ridiculous. Its intimidating geography, its uncompromising climates, and its built-in divisions have been constants in Canadian history. Many years ago, before radio and television satellites provided a crucial electronic bond for Canada's parts, they prompted one traveling lecturer to title his talks on Canada "The Landless Man and Manless Land."

With a few notable exceptions such as nineteenth-century insurrections or the noisy mailbox bombs of a few men and women seeking independence for Quebec in the 1960's and 1970's, Canada's confrontations have been more verbal than violent. Canadians have been too busy merely surviving to take time to tame the land.

Comfortable Obscurity?

Canadians have tended to shrink from grand continental concepts like the Americans struggling over their Wild West, Australians fighting over the Outback, or Brazilians wrestling with (and damaging) the riches of the Amazon. As a group, Canadians have tended to prefer their shy obscurity to any loud claims of national achievement, which would be seen as too boastfully American.

But now as a more mature nation, Canadians of all backgrounds are struggling and conquering and wrestling with their own undeveloped country. And in this effort they are simultaneously beginning to broaden their own individual and collective national horizons with a

The Mackenzie River Delta in the Northwest Territories. The Mackenzie River is one of the largest rivers in the Western hemisphere. Government of Canada, ISTC

An Automated Tunnel

For decades the Canadian Pacific Railway has run only one line through the imposing Rocky Mountains. Sometimes it could be closed for days by landslides or avalanches. Always it was limited in train capacity, first because only one train could be moved through at a time (only 15 per day), and second, because the uphill struggle was so great for westbound trains that six extra 3,000-horsepower diesel engines had to be added in the middle and rear of the 115-car trains. Even then, the powerful engines could nudge the 14,000-ton train along at only 10 miles an hour.

Building the first line in the 1800's was considered a major feat, but adding another was an even greater accomplishment, and an urgent one given the rapidly growing exports, especially grains, that Canada was exporting to the developing countries around the Pacific rim in the 1980's. The task involved laying about 22 miles (35 kilometers) of new track through rugged mountains, including constructing a 9.1-mile-long tunnel straight through one massive mountain. It would take about a decade of work and $500 million (Canadian) and it would mean 24 trains a day were possible.

The track involved new bridges and laying rails along steep mountainsides. But it reduced the climbing grade from 2.2 percent (2.2 feet up for every 100 feet of track ahead) to 1 percent. But then came the tunnel work. Two different companies began at opposite sides of the mountain and, using modern engineering methods, their separate borings met near the middle only a few inches off.

But that was just the beginning. Tunnels can be almost any

length themselves, but the equipment has to be able to get through. Diesels give off immense amounts of fumes and heat; one engine in one minute gives off about 280,000 British thermal units, enough to take nearly 200 gallons of water from freezing to the boiling point. Such heat and exhaust would overwhelm the other engines, not to mention the crews.

Canadian Pacific's engineers came up with an ingenious solution involving a series of fans and doors at the tunnel ends and midpoint. When a westbound train enters the tunnel, a door just beyond the middle closes off the western half of the tunnel; huge fans above the tunnel's midpoint blow fresh air into the tunnel at the oncoming train while a fan at the eastern end sucks the used air out (and vice versa for eastbound trains). The airflow must be carefully regulated; too little air lets the engines overheat, and too much would actually slow the train and make the engines work harder.

When the train reaches the middle, the door opens until the cars pass. Then it closes to allow the fans, themselves sitting atop the mountain on a 1,150-foot-tall, 28-foot-diameter (345 meters × 8.4 meters) air shaft, to clean the eastern half while fresh air is sucked in from the western end to continue the cooling effect. Interestingly, even at 2,250 horsepower the five fans do only half the work. The simple motion of the train moving through the narrow tunnel like a piston in a car's cylinder forces more air past the engines.*

*John Holusha, "Overcoming Limits to Rail Tunnels," *The New York Times*, May 10, 1989, p. D10.

new kind of self-confidence in achieving success rather than simply surviving. Canada's harsh physical reality and climate has been a blessing in many ways, and Canadians are using it to profit, to preserve, and to train themselves. For while it spawned pessimism in many Canadians (things are going to get a whole lot worse, many seemed to expect, before they go completely bad), the land also instilled a sense of realism and acceptance in their national personality. It is now becoming apparent that it has also bred a kind of toughness, tenacity, and reliability that is not learned from schoolbooks. Now, instead of being intimidated by their environment, instead of seeing limits in the scale and harshness of their land, many Canadians are seeing it as a teacher. And they are using it as an opportunity to test new skills and handle new challenges.

Survival Skills

The Shield may look forbidding, but it has also provided a wilderness camp for groups of business executives and even teens to test their survival skills in one- or two-week sessions designed for them to learn more about teamwork, trust, and themselves. The Shield is also a treasure trove of natural resources. Canada's lakes and bogs still yield a valuable annual harvest in furs. The same waters formed a crude waterway for the canoes of early traders and nowadays an isolated playground for fishers, swimmers, campers, and other tourists, many of them foreigners eager to flee their hectic lives in more southerly civilizations. The Shield's ground yields 40 percent of Canada's mineral production as well as abundant woods for lumber, firewood, and pulp for the world's paper industry, including much of the paper in many American newspapers. These wild waters also give Canada the ability to make vast amounts of hydroelectricity, electricity generated by the power of falling water. This power, or hydro, as many Canadians call it, provides some 70 percent of Canada's electricity.

Canoeing rapids on the Seal River, northern Manitoba. The Seal is slated to become part of the Canadian Heritage River System.   Rod Beebe/SportsLight

Building a Nation

In recent times southern Canadians have begun to appreciate more and to use their special northernness instead of resisting it. As Canadian companies grow larger and become more national in scope, their employees are promoted and transferred, then routinely travel back and forth across the country. The federal government even helped fund "foreign" student exchanges between Canadian provinces. All this helped to break down ignorance and stereotypes, which go together.

Instead of just fishing and hunting for themselves, Indian bands have tapped their isolated reserves as lucrative attractions for city fishers eager to flee urban pressures, sounds, and smells. This brought new income to many families and businesses. Instead of bemoaning the long winters, some small-scale farmers around Yellowknife, Northwest Terri-

Some Different School Lessons

Since the 1950's most of Canada's once-nomadic Inuit have been gathered together into villages where government services like health and education can be more easily administered. There have been considerable cultural gaps and misunderstandings as a modern welfare state such as Canada comes in contact with an ancient, established society such as the Inuit, whose culture had to be portable enough to fit on a sled. But in a typical Canadian gesture of compromise with a nod to the climatological realities, the school year and day in northern Canada are determined by the local community and by the harsh climate.

Each Arctic school can schedule its 190 required days of classes whenever it wants, because local traditions and hunting patterns vary greatly and the pull of the wild is so great that without such flexibility many families would not stay around for their children to attend school.

In Resolute, Northwest Territories, for instance, three full-time teachers handle about 50 pupils. With the agreement of the town's 177 residents, the Resolute school year runs from late August, which is autumn in the Arctic, until late May, which is spring. The school day runs from about 7:30 until 2:30, with breaks for recess and a hot lunch. During much of the winter, of course, there is no sunlight, while during summer vacation the sun never sets. Although winter temperatures regularly run at $-20°F$ ($-28°C$) outdoor play is very popular, although it may be canceled if the neighborhood's polar bears have been seen recently.

There are no evil strangers to warn the children against, but there are signs about the bears: "ATTENTION! The hand that feeds could get eaten." And there is a large picture of a very large polar bear who bears no resemblance whatsoever to his friendly southern cousin, Smokey. "Bears are dangerous. They are bigger and faster than you are. Don't feed them," reads another. Polar bears are indeed tough. One swipe of their huge paws can knock the head off a seal.

Teaching and learning in Arctic schools is complicated by language. The Inuit children speak English only during school hours. At home the family speaks Inuktitut. The native language is on the radio, too, at times, and the local television channel. But the majority of broadcasts that shower down on Canada's north from an array of satellites hovering 22,300 miles overhead are in English. Many Arctic homes leave the television on around the clock. One community, Igloolik, voted against allowing any television sets, so concerned were the adults that their traditional values would be corrupted by the modern medium. Indeed, many teachers found considerable confusion among some children who would never see a real horse, but could see some on TV that seemed to talk, as well as automobiles that flew and people who shot guns at each other.

The Resolute school's principal, Mike Pembroke, had to make many adjustments. When he scheduled his first parents' night at the school for the teachers to discuss children's grades, only three people showed up, and they were all teachers. The other parents were too shy to come out. So now after every report card Mr. Pembroke, the teacher, and an interpreter troop around the settlement from student's house to student's house, calling on each family to pass the time of day, sip tea, and slip in some polite comments here and there on their child's academic progress. "They don't seem to care much about the grades," Mr. Pembroke said. "But they are interested in their child's behavior. And there is a marked improvement for a couple of weeks after every meeting."

Mr. Pembroke also adjusts the curriculum to account for some special local needs. Each winter he hires some local men for a week or two to take his older male students out "onto the land," as the Inuit put it. The aging men perform the informal survival instruction that had been traditionally provided by fathers as the family wandered about the land. Now, in settlements, the fathers have seen their authority wither. The young men learn how to make igloos, which can save their lives in a sudden Arctic storm. They are taught sled making, how to tell directions by the way the snow blows, where to find seal air holes for better hunting, how to read what lies over the horizon by reading cloud reflections and, very importantly, which ice is old enough to be free of salt and safe to melt for drinking.

One day these wise old instructors let their students learn the hard way about Arctic tides. When the students chose one spot to drill a hole through six feet of ice, the men did not object. But an hour later, when the students' drill broke through, there was no water. Beneath the ice the tide had gone out while the students drilled.

It was a special lesson they would not soon forget.

tories, have begun using the 24-hour summer days to grow melons. Using an old nickel mine far beneath Sudbury, Ontario, scientists are putting the earth's steady 55-degree temperature to use growing vegetables in artificial light. Instead of hibernating indoors for the long northern Alberta winter, small businessmen like Jacques Van Pelt launched tourist businesses to take southerners on overnight dogsled journeys into a real wilderness to see wild buffalo or, in the summer, thousands of wild birds. In eastern Canada, engineers have erected underwater "windmills" to harness the vast electrical generating potential of the twice-daily shifting of the waters in Canada's tidal basins. Instead of fighting the ice, exploration crews use its strength to hold huge cement caissons in place, forming temporary humanmade islands to drill for oil and gas in the Beaufort Sea and Arctic Ocean.

Ice Rigs

Other crews drill small holes in the Arctic Ocean ice above spots that seem to promise possible oil and gas reserves. For many days a steady stream of ocean water is pumped up through that hole and sent spilling across a mile or more of ice, already several feet thick. The result, in those temperatures of minus 40 degrees, is that the ice gradually grows thicker. It creates an upside-down dome of ice twenty-five or more feet thick. This ice has not only enough strength but enough buoyancy to support a 5.5-million-pound oil-drilling rig.

The gangly rigs come in out of the sky, more than 120 planeloads for every rig. Their drills pierce first the ice, then glide through perhaps 500 feet or more of icy water to grind their way through two or three miles of rock and sediment, probing for the resources that someday may light distant homes or fuel faraway vehicles. All the while, these temporary floating towns and their 40 or 50 residents are supplied by more airfreighters, which bank out of the black sky at all hours to land on runways made of ice and lighted by long strings of 100-watt bulbs.

When spring comes, crews cap the holes or wells. Using satellites far above, they precisely position the operations on their maps or leave small underwater radio transmitters to beep out weak little signals until drilling crews return to resume drilling the next autumn. The same planes wheel in from above to land on the now-weakening ice. They

Oil companies actively search for oil and gas in the Arctic. The dogs do their best to keep polar bears away from the site, or at least bark warnings of their approach. Canapress Photo Service

pack up the entire rig again in load after load and take off down the now-slushy runways. Sometimes they cut it so close to the sudden Arctic spring thaw that the heavy planes can't land and the oil rigs must be slowly hauled off the ice in convoys of trucks creeping many miles along the ocean surface in water up to their hubcaps.

It is the kind of quiet, little-noticed courage that Canadians excel at. Some 2,500 miles away, however, in the thin band of land near the United States that is populated Canada, hardly anyone pays attention. It is the kind of achievement that Canadians take so much for granted.

The First
Canadians

In the beginning, there was no border, no proprietary names. There were only the native peoples and the abundance of wildlife that made their existence possible. For these people there was no Canada nor a United States. For them, the only lines drawn were by the rivers, the migratory patterns of the game, and the changes in the seasons.

Some time more than 15,000 years ago, bands of hardy Asian nomads are believed to have drifted, on foot and in fragile boats, across the narrow land bridge where the Bering Strait now is, from Asia to the North American mainland.

Over many centuries they wandered south and east across the Americas in search of food and shelter. They developed many different languages and customs, and honed their skills in making tools, developing social organization, creating art, and simply surviving on what, in Canada, was then and remains now a harsh landscape.

Cooperation and Community

Their societies adapted to the land and the wildlife, stressing pragmatism and cooperation. Their communities were never very large by modern standards, totaling only about 220,000 throughout Canada when the first Europeans arrived. Being too large would have meant that a community could not support itself on the often meager foods available; most communities also had to be portable so they could follow the migrating game, especially in the far north where the few weeks of frost-free summer days were too short to allow cultivation of crops. Even much farther south, on the harsh but more hospitable Canadian prairies, the natives followed the instinctive wanderings of animals such as the buffalo. Those bands of natives who did settle long enough to cultivate crops found themselves forced to move every few years as the fertility of fields was exhausted. One exception is the Hurons, who were farmers.

Knowing the Land

All these native groups were very wise in the ways of the wild whose land they respected and whose spirits they worshipped. Hunting and killing animals was never an idle sport. To kill more animals than necessary for their group to share and survive was not only wasteful but disrespectful of the animal spirits who, the natives believed, offered themselves to the hunters as part of a delicate balance in nature. So, for instance, coming upon a wild bird's nest full of eggs, a native hunter would always leave several eggs untouched to assure there would be more birds to lay more eggs to be eaten in the future.

As some groups of Asian immigrants filtered across the expanses of northern North America, they became the tribes of Indians and bands of Inuit whose descendants survive on these same lands today. The Inuit live in the frigid Arctic, where winter nights last all day and summer days last all night, and the Indians live to the south below the treeline.

Old Problems, New Solutions   Canada's natives have gone through many difficult changes since their first encounters, not always friendly, with European explorers. And while their health and formal education have improved greatly in the years since the government began paying greater attention to these minorities around 1950, Canada's Inuit and Indian cultures have undergone some of the same drastic and often painful changes as have Native Americans as they adapt to government requirements and modern pressures on traditional cultures.

A new, more assertive generation of native Canadian leaders is fast emerging and is in the process of negotiating agreements leading to a more independent relationship with a more conscientious federal gov-

The Inuit hold their own Arctic Winter Games with new and traditional events. This is being held at Yellowknife in the Northwest Territories.   Government of Canada, ISTC

An Original Canadian

He stands five feet tall in his caribou-skin boots. His hands are dark and wide, the skin thick like well-worn leather. He wears a battered baseball cap, though he's never heard of that sport. His name is Napoleon Snowbird Martin. He has lived in the Canadian bush of northeastern Alberta and the Northwest Territories since near the beginning of this century.

Snowbird is unable to read words on paper. But he can read tracks and blood in the snow and branches broken certain ways and sounds in the wild air. He knows the colors of good clouds and bad clouds and the sunsets and different winds that predict tomorrow's weather. And he can speak four languages—Cree, English, Chipewyan, and dog—sometimes all in the same sentence. "I'm seventy-seven years old," he says. "I'm just beginning to grow."

Snowbird is one of a few Canadian natives who still run dogs. Most have changed to snowmobiles, which can go farther faster through their frozen countryside. Snowmobiles don't get sick with worms. They don't fight each other. But dogs don't break down in the woods, far from help. All they want are a couple of frozen fish to crunch up whole every day, frequent mouthfuls of snow along the route, and the chance to hear Snowbird's reassuring voice behind them as the 600-pound (275-kilogram) sled whispers its way across the snow.

Snowbird reads their moods through tail signals, cocked ears, and wiggled noses. He knows the instincts behind certain howls or growls, when a fight is about to erupt. According to Snowbird's philosophy: "Dogs can't live without love. Like people."

The animals—all males to avoid any amorous rivalries—know how to read Snowbird, too. They know what *click-click, hup,* and *jah* mean. They know that two or three of them trying to grab a mouthful of snow on the run prompts Snowbird to call a rest stop for a longer "drink." They know it means trouble when Snowbird breaks off a handy branch and strides forward, muttering. But they read, too, the abiding affection in Snowbird's voice, regardless of their English meaning. "This dog something you call dumb," he said, smiling, as he lifted a misplaced leg back into the harness. The dog gave Snowbird a lick of appreciation.

"Okay, boys," he said, "*click-click hup* now *jah*" (translation: "Let's go, get going now to the left"). Even when the trail is obvious, Snowbird keeps up his nonstop banter. "They like to hear me here," he said, not mentioning how much he likes it, too. Then he whistled. "*Hapsiko hup chee chee*, let's go, don't get crazy, boys, watch out, I kill you and eat you, *click*, keep quiet you."

Snowbird will teach visitors some Cree words: *dahnsi* (hello), *atim* (dog), *peahtik* (look out), *hay-hay* (yes), *nehmoyeh* (no), *kaynana-skoh-mitten* (thank you), *etah-tohm-skah-gan* (good-bye), and, Snowbird's favorite, *aygotah* (you betcha, man).

In his life, it is necessary to have eight words for different kinds of ice but mechanical timepieces like watches are unnecessary. Minutes and hours are too confining and hard to measure. Snowbird and his friends deal in seasons or periods of sunlight and darkness, which makes sense since trappers do not punch a time clock on their way to work. Time to Snowbird is something to spend, not conserve. And energy and personal resources must be conserved for the hard times which, experience has taught him, will surely come someday. City folks carry a spare tire in the car trunk; Snowbird packs extra food on his dogsled. It is a very Canadian thing to do.

He believes the important elements of life include respect for nature, for being part of nature not its master, for being another creature wandering the earth, not a wasteful intruder. He will cut down a tree for wood and hunt animals for food, but never for fun. Canadians are very much aware of their environment and humanmade threats to it.

Snowbird remembers when he and his friends spent all summer getting ready for winter and all winter trapping, hunting, and cutting wood to last until summer, year after year. "In old days," he said, as he crunched along a frozen river in his sled, "people live all down this river in sheds and tents. They fish and hunt and trap. All Cree. Now all gone. They don't move to town. They move down into ground. All dead. Some sick. Some get funny, you know. Some just die. I sick once. They say flu, something like that. Long time ago. I don't remember what time that is."

And things have changed in the wild. "Today," Snowbird said, "young people go in bush, they get lost. They don't listen to fathers, and fathers don't try teach. Always drinking and stuff like that. Now buy everything from store. I don't know why—crazy or lazy, I guess."

Sometimes at night around a campfire, when the winds are gentle

ernment. Indeed, it was a Cree leader and provincial legislator, Elijah Harper, whose filibuster, rooted in frustration over delays in these negotiations, fatally torpedoed the Meech Lake Accord in 1990. The accord, designed to give more recognition and independence to Quebec, did not address similar native desires. The agreements call for more native representation in government and formally setting aside vast areas of land for native ownership all over the country, other areas for partial rights (such as the right to hunt), and promising payment of hundreds of millions of dollars to the natives over the next ten to fifteen

and the dogs are howling back at a wolf they will never see, Snowbird will finish his dinner of duck or rabbit, buffalo or caribou, or sometimes muskrat, with instant potatoes, powdered drinks, and a muffin. "Good food," he says. "Now I have power for two days."

Then he may tell a tale that Cree grandfathers have told for thousands of years since the glaciers left those northern plains open and cratered with thousands of ponds and lakes as homes for countless animals and, thus, one of the world's richest fur grounds. It is the tale of an old Indian, blind and unable to hunt for his own food, a terrible fate. The old man was sitting sadly by the lake when a loon approached. " 'Hang on to my neck like this and come swim with me,' " Snowbird said the bird said. And the old man did. Three times the bird dived under the water. And three times the man opened his eyes there. And when they surfaced the third time, the clean Canadian waters had done their healing job. And the forces of nature, the hunter and the hunted, were back in balance. The man could see. "He could hunt once more for his own food," said Snowbird. "It is a true story."

years. These sums, paid in return for forfeiting all rights to other lands, will go toward raising the standard of living and helping to establish and support an array of ongoing native businesses so that families and communities can become more self-supporting.

These agreements, which together total more than $1.5 billion and involve 40 percent of Canada's entire land mass, will finally clear up more than a century of confusion and conflict over what land and rights belong to the natives and what Canada's larger responsibilities are to its indigenous minorities. While to some the agreements unfortunately further divide a country already divided by many forces, the official certainty of these legal agreements is also likely to encourage more outside business investment in Canada's isolated areas, including multi-billion-dollar pipelines and resource developments. "This," said Richard Van Loon, a senior federal official, "is probably the largest property transfer without bloodshed in history."*

Woodland Peoples

Although some of the languages and customs of the native groups were similar, these were mostly distinct societies of drifting bands shaped in large part by the varying landscapes they inhabited. The eight major woodland tribes, for instance, lived in eastern and parts of central Canada and included the Micmacs, the now-extinct Beothuks, the Cree, and the Ojibway, sometimes called the Chippewa. They relied heavily on trees, using moss to line bedding of fir boughs and sheets of bark stitched together with thin tree roots to construct canoes light enough to carry between lakes. Wood was also used for eating utensils and for building natural-looking fences and other obstacles along animal trails to silently guide the prey toward a trap or waiting hunter.

Iroquois
On the other hand, the Iroquois, actually an alliance of several tribes such as the Mohawk, the Oneida, the Cayuga, and the Seneca, inhabited the rich, broad lands of southern Ontario. They were excellent farmers, which gave their society a stability denied the more nomadic bands. Farming (corn, beans, squash, sunflowers) provided most of their diet, eliminating the time-consuming daily hunt for animals. Such a life gave them popular products for trading and also more leisure time to make war on neighbors, which could earn a young man

*Paul Lewis, "Canada About to Sign Major Land Agreement with Eskimos," *The New York Times* (August 21, 1989), p. A3.

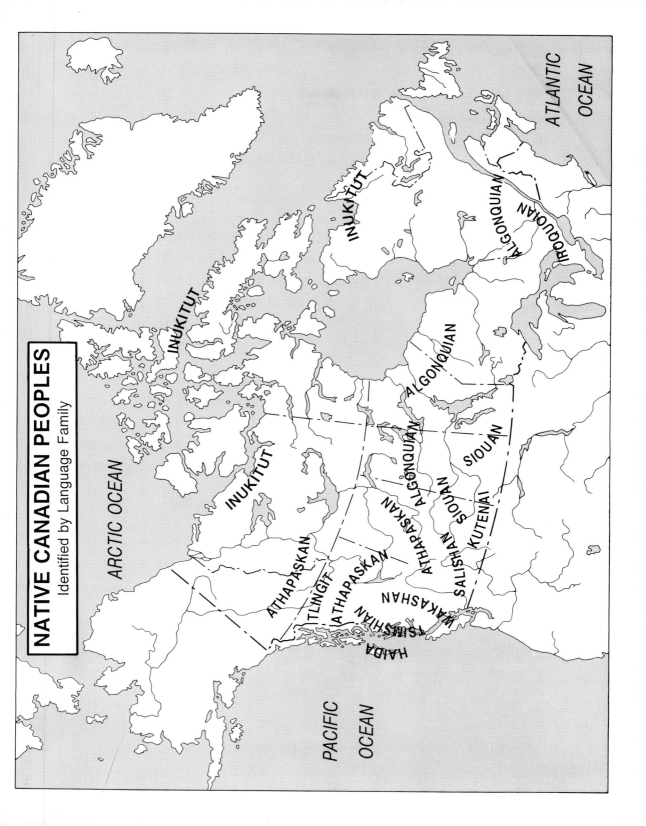

NATIVE CANADIAN PEOPLES
Identified by Language Family

ARCTIC OCEAN

ATLANTIC OCEAN

PACIFIC OCEAN

INUKITUT

INUKITUT

INUKITUT

ALGONQUIAN

ALGONQUIAN

ALGONQUIAN

IROQUOIAN

SIOUAN

SIOUAN

ATHAPASKAN

ATHAPASKAN

ATHAPASKAN

TLINGIT

HAIDA

TSIMSHIAN

WAKASHAN

SALISHAN

KUTENAI

considerable prestige. Of course, among the attacked communities, this also created the need to seek revenge in counterattacks. And all this, in turn, led to the need to fortify their semipermanent settlements of 100 to 1,000 members who lived, several families together, in large, wooden longhouses.

These confederacies of tribes also provided sophisticated systems of government, with two chiefs presiding—one for civil affairs and another for military matters. But the advice of all elders and a general consensus was vital in virtually all matters.

Blackfoot and Other Plains Indians   Canada's Plains Indians—tribes such as the Blackfoot, Blood, Piegan, Plains Cree, and Sioux—had to prize mobility, sometimes migrating into what was to become the United States. This made horses as well as lightweight, easily disassembled housing a valuable asset; hence the evolution of the tipi, a circular network of wooden poles leaning into each other and wrapped in layers of animal skins. But these tipis had other clever design features; the back walls were steeper than the front, for example, which provided more room in the location accorded to the household head. But the slight tilt of the tipi also improved ventilation through a smoke hole at the top where the poles joined. The tilt also gave the structure added strength, as it could "lean" into the prevailing prairie winds.

Out in the open prairies where trees were absent and quarry could see figures approaching for miles, Plains hunters erected clusters of converging bushes along animal trails, forcing the creatures into ever-narrower paths within range of hunters' arrows. At times hunters on horseback would capture a group of buffalo by surrounding them and making the circle smaller and smaller. Sometimes herds of buffalo could be caught by stampeding them off cliffs, called "jumps." Virtually every

George Catlin's nineteenth-century drawing of an Indian buffalo hunt. National
Archives of Canada/Negative no. C 47226

part of the fallen animal was used—the skin, after laborious drying, treatment, and rubbing, became clothing, bedding, and footwear; the sinew went into sewing; the meat was food. Even dried buffalo droppings were collected and burned to provide vital cooking fires and wintertime heat.

By necessity, hunting on such a scale was a cooperative group effort and the proceeds were shared according to family needs, with special charitable allotments made for the elderly and ill. Some of the meat was dried in thin strips and then pounded into a long-lasting nutritious powder and mixed with fat. Called pemmican, it could easily last for years and be carried when traveling.

Fighting occurred during raids to steal other tribes' horses, to protect hunting or sacred territories, and in small-scale skirmishes designed less for killing than to earn courage points for attacking warriors. Until the introduction of firearms by Europeans, weapons were primarily bows and arrows, clubs, and stone-tipped spears and knives.

Coastal Indians

Canada's western and coastal Indians, including the Interior Salish, the Lillooet, the Shushwap, the Okanagan, and Kootenay, the Haida, the Tsimshian, Gitskan, Nootka, Coast Salish, and Bella Coola, also had animal-skin tipis; but in more mountainous areas some lived in underground caves, while in virgin forest areas large wooden structures were popular. Living by large rivers and the Pacific Ocean, having portable canoes was not so important. So canoes were heavy hollowed-out tree trunks with tall bows added on to prevent ocean waves from swamping the craft. Some were large enough to carry a crew of eight.

Fish, much of it dried and saved for winter nourishment, played a far more important food role, along with mountain berries and tasty slivers of inner bark from evergreen trees and poplars. Fish were caught using spears, nets made of woven grasses or tree roots, or simple stone dams that trapped the creatures long enough for spearing. Fish by-products were also important. Fish oil, for instance, was an important dietary supplement, and some oils could be burned for light.

A few coastal tribes also hunted larger sea life such as sea otters, sea lions, and whales. Using heavy harpoons with sharp shell fragments for tips and whittled antler tips for barbs, these hunters had to get very near their prey. Towing a whale carcass home could take several days, but arrival was cause for a great celebration and divvying up of the animal according to tribal rank.

Since chasing migrating food was not necessary, more permanent settlements, housing, and heavier furnishings developed, including elaborately decorated wooden chests. Such chests and intricately carved totem poles recounting a family's exploits and heritage could be a sign of great prestige. Indeed, some coastal Indian groupings had clearly defined social levels of nobles, commoners, and slaves, who were usually prisoners of war. Sometimes even these rankings contained other layers of social standing.

The Indians imbued their hunting prey with spirits. Northern tribes, for instance, strictly followed ritual hunting and butchering techniques to display their respect for the game. Pacific coast tribes thought that salmon were really supernatural creatures who lived in the sea and changed into fish to offer themselves as food to humans. So respected were these large fish and so eager were the Indians to assure their reappearance that every salmon bone was returned to the water to ensure the fish's resurrection.

Inuit

About ten basic groupings of Inuit with twenty different dialects inhabited Canada's far north. These groups included the Mackenzie Inuit along the Mackenzie River in the western Arctic, the Caribou Inuit along the west coast of Hudson Bay, the Igloolik Inuit to the north, the South Baffin Island Inuit, the Ungava Inuit in northern Quebec, and the Labrador Inuit along Canada's eastern Arctic coast. Few groups had access to wood, though some copper was utilized in some areas.

As with the Indians, the traditional life of Canada's Inuit was built around the search for food, whether it was fishing, hunting larger sea animals from animal-skin kayaks, or wandering far afield in dogsleds searching for caribou and other game. Meat could be stored in home-made freezers deep within a pile of rocks doused with water that quickly froze. But animals provided more than just food. Bird bones became

A Strange Tale in Two Tongues

Herb Zimmerman *Nohtsi enitl'e-cho dok'e wots'ikw'o ha tlichoyati k'alaiwo.* Or to put it another way, Herb Zimmerman is translating the Bible into an Indian language, Dogrib.

It is quite a challenge. The language of the Northwest Territories' small Dogrib tribe (so named because they believe God created the first Indian from a dog's rib) is an irregular language that had never been written, although to many its guttural sounds and consonants are reminiscent of the Navajo language. First, Mr. Zimmerman and his wife, Judy, who are missionaries, had to learn the language. Then they had to divine what its unwritten rules were and then devise a way to write it phonetically. Then came translating the Bible's ancient stories and images into a culture where the concepts, for instance, of kings or shepherds do not exist.

The Zimmermans were concerned that only 3,000 people still speak Dogrib, and half of them have also learned English. Besides the vocabulary (eight words for different kinds of ice) and the grammar (pronouns go in the middle of the verb), the Zimmermans also had to learn Indian manners. It is considered rude, they discovered, for a newcomer to wait for an invitation to a neighbor's house. One must make an immediate "walk around" from house to house, paying your respects first to the chief and then the elders. They spent countless hours simply socializing and working with the Indians to earn their trust. And they learned the hard way about misunderstandings between cultures. An early draft translation of the Easter story drew guffaws when it included a word for simply inserting the cross in the sand instead of one for formally erecting the cross.

Some terms, like "public baths," required explanatory footnotes, since even private baths are not a part of the Dogrib daily ritual. The Three Wise Men became three chiefs. An exotic animal like the camel became simply a horse.

And Dogrib has no word for a spiritual brother; in the language there can only be brothers who are older, younger, or twins, and anyone outside the family cannot possibly be a brother. So to write an appropriate explanation, the Zimmermans had to do considerable research into Biblical families.

There were other hurdles that revealed much about Indian life. With the tribe's strong sense of sharing and community property, possessives can apply only to a person's body or relatives, like "my arm" or "my father" and never "my gun" or "my sled." Such inanimate objects must go into prepositional phrases such as "this sled is to me."

Mr. Zimmerman also had to contend with several words for different kinds of white men: *qwheti* ("stone-house people"), *molah* ("people with many buttons on their clothes"—that is, the French-Canadian trappers who passed through), and *beicho* ("big knife people," or the Americans with their oversize Bowie knives). Although all Dogribs live within 200 miles of each other, they have evolved regional dialects. In Yellowknife, in the Northwest Territories, for instance, an airplane is *tseta,* but just 5 miles away in Rae it is *enitl'ek'et'a*, literally "paper plane," recalling early canvas-covered aircraft.

One major problem involved adequately translating the word and concept of "shepherd" with its spiritual connotation of caring for a dependent flock. Dogribs don't raise animals in domestic herds; they hunt wild ones; and when they find them they kill them. So Mr. Zimmerman settled on the word *gikedi* ("one who cares for people"), although it is usually used only for communal baby-sitters.

Here is an example of how one Biblical passage appears in English and Dogrib, along with the literal translation of the Dogrib. It is Mark 6:34: "And Jesus, when he came out, saw much people, and was moved with compassion toward them, because they were as sheep not having a shepherd: and He began to teach them many things."

Zezi ka-atla ko do hlo ni-ideh goai
("Jesus came out when people many they were there he saw them")

etege-et'i gonihwo
("they are pitiful is how he felt toward them")

sahzoa gikedi hwile lagit'e t'a
("sheep one who cares for them was missing that is how they were since")

Hani niwo t'a t'asi hlo t'a hoghagoreto
("That way he felt since things many he taught them").

sewing needles. Whalebones became sled runners. Caribou skin from the tough forehead became shoe soles. The softer underbelly skin made good socks, while the rest went into kayaks (one- or two-man canoes) or umiaks (larger open boats). Animal skins also became parkas or the walls of tents, which housed families in the less frigid summer. Winter housing was often blocks of ice cleverly arranged into igloos, hollow ice domes that resisted the long winter's fierce winds.

Hunting required great skill—memorizing a landscape that can seem barren and featureless to some, knowing when and where certain types of animals gathered, how to approach them undetected on the open Arctic tundra. Hunting also required great patience, crouching for many hours on the open ice by a seal's breathing hole waiting for the animal to stick its nose up for air. The Inuit's concept of time was different, too. Meals, for example, did not come at set times because food wasn't always available. When available, *muktuk* (whale skin and blubber) was especially popular.

Different families, united through adoption or marriage, cooperated closely on the hunt, on erecting housing, on caring for the children. Because anyone who could not help was a burden and a threat to survival, the elderly and sick were often killed or left behind to die. And male babies were more highly prized because they would become hunters.

Women's duties included child care, making housing, gathering berries and seaweed, and making the family's clothing. Hunters could require five pairs of boots every winter, but Inuit custom associated calamity with preparing caribou skin or meat while out on the ice. So a family's entire winter wardrobe would have to be finished before they moved onto the ice each winter.

Like the Indians, the Inuit relied on shamans, or informal priests, as intermediaries with the spirits of nature they worshipped. Shamans would divine what was causing a lack of animals for hunting, and what rituals would correct the situation. They were also believed to possess healing powers.

For entertainment, the Inuit had many games from hide-and-seek and pretend-hunting to arm wrestling, high kicking, and cat's cradle, all of which encouraged some skill such as agility or imaginative thinking. Cat's cradle, for instance, involved stretching a circle of sinew between a player's two hands. Using their fingers, players created a series of loops and designs resembling animals, which other players would try to duplicate. Although there was no written Inuit language until nineteenth-century missionaries designed a special alphabet, story-telling was entertainment and a means to pass on values, philosophies, and family history.

And although art for art's sake was not a common feature of life, in their long hours waiting out storms many Inuit developed sophisticated skills in carving stone, bone, and whale ivory. Some became utensils and tools. But often the objects portrayed local animals and were purely decorative.

Watched by his wife and son, an Inuk hunter skins a wolf for sale or clothing.   Fred Bruemmer

Modern Times

With no formal schools for most of their history, skills such as hunting, sled making, navigating on the ice and in storms, butchering, sewing, cooking, and even carving were efficiently taught by parents, grandparents, and community elders, who derived much social standing and personal satisfaction from this role. This was inadvertently disrupted after 1950 as the federal government focused overdue attention on the health, education, and welfare of the Inuit, who now total about 28,000 in Canada.

Many nomadic Inuit were herded into government housing in static communities where old ways came under new pressures. The new communities and new ways, underwritten by the government, brought improved health, formal education, transportation, and communication. But it also brought cigarettes, candy, television, and the devastating social effects of alcohol, drugs, and affluence on a proud, primitive culture where survival was once the best that could be hoped for. Children have drifted from the old ways without fully understanding the new. The elderly were taken from the old ways perhaps without wanting the new. The result is a morass of conflicting cultures and social values, often within the same household.

Teenage children, for example, were flown out to live at regional high schools hundreds of miles away, where instructors from southern Canada imposed a kind of discipline entirely different from that of the youngsters' extended families at home. When the graduates returned to their isolated communities, wiser in the ways of the world and, by traditional standards, less respectful of old ways, they were prepared to earn a living in an economy that did not exist in their tiny towns but were unprepared to survive on the land as their ancestors had.

Recently, the government has combatted these problems by, in part, helping to train more Inuit teachers and by giving more decision-making

Divining What's Inside a Stone

Tagoonarak is uncertain how old he is, where he was born, or how his name is spelled in the English alphabet. But he is sure of one thing: He loves to carve.

Five days a week this man, who is at least 85, rises before dawn and moves slowly down to the art room of the regional high school in Iqualuit, formerly called Frobisher Bay, on Baffin Island. There he joins some friends in hours of sawing, filing, and polishing rough stone in the likeness of the creatures they all used to hunt. But before starting come hours of study, turning the stone over and over in his leathery hands.

"I try to sense," said Alivuktuk, another elderly carver, "what kind of spirit is inside trying to get out."

The results are primitive by some standards. Details are few, and facial features are often scratched in. But the simplicity is striking. Humans, always portrayed in everyday tasks, are never smiling and are frequently leaning, as if laboring under a heavy load or into a strong wind.

"It is hard to describe the pleasure," added Alivuktuk through an interpreter. "You see, I hunted all these animals for many years. I came to know them well. We lived together on the land. And from seeking them all before, I know how to carve them, although I still

powers to local citizens. New, forceful groups of natives, financed by government grants, have also emerged to make the Inuit case, as in the land claims negotiations.

With the replacement of simple kayaks and reliable dogsled teams by faster motorboats and snowmobiles, fishing, trapping, and hunting

have trouble with caribou. The legs are very difficult unless they are lying down."

Carving, once merely a pastime, is now also an organized escape from some modern realities for carvers like Alivuktuk, Tagoonarak, Ayapow, and Jamasee Ishulugak. "The younger generation is no longer interested in carving," said Alivuktuk, who is 71 and learned how to hunt, survive on the land, and carve from his father. "The young ones, they just watch that television, stay out late, sleep in late, and ask for more money whenever they feel like it."

But he says no money could buy the joy he gets from carving among his friends, from creating something with his hands, from the memories of long-ago hunts and the tales the carvers swap by the hour in Inuktitut as they chip, file, and smooth away the stone and bone of yet another creature from their imagination.

So great are the skills of these leisure-time artisans in observing animal behavior and translating it with their hands that a carved stone bird can sit on the table, looking lifelike and frozen in fear, with its head cocked slightly as if it just heard the approaching viewer.

These carvings, now marketed through native cooperatives, have become very popular—and very expensive—as art objects around the world. Skillful making of colorful lithographs depicting village or hunting scenes has also provided vital income for many Inuit.

became more expensive. So did the supplies of manufactured foods and fuels shipped north on cargo ships that arrive but once every year. Anything else has to come on even more expensive airlifts. So while it may be possible for one person to live off the land, it is very difficult to support a family this way.

Government health care has reduced infant mortality. But this has also led to larger families, which hinder nomadic movements and require more income to feed and clothe. Improved health care also leads to longer life expectancy, which means a greater burden for young families supporting their parents and in-laws.

A Shared Nation

Although by and large Canada has dealt and is dealing with its native minority populations more humanely than some other countries, the combination of modern Europeans with their weapons and utensils along with some customs and diseases that proved particularly debilitating were too powerful a pressure for the fragmented and less technologically advanced societies. The Indians and Inuit did, however, play a vital, historic role in the making of Canada. Many tribes were intimately involved in the successful military defense of Canada during the American Revolution and the War of 1812. And the natives proved to be invaluable teachers of survival to the more numerous Europeans trying to surmount North America's trackless distances. Without Indian and Inuit lessons in wilderness travel by water and across deep snows, and in finding and making shelter, clothing, and foods including corn, Canada's modern industrial welfare state would not have been possible.

New, more modern political and business systems and expertise are emerging within the Inuit and Indian communities to provide new channels of achievement, earning power, self-esteem, and satisfaction. But it is a long, slow process.

Becoming
a Nation

The North American continent was one land to its native people. Initially, it was even one land to the European explorers who happened upon its eastern coast. Many similar threads run throughout the early histories of Canada and the United States, but they have gone into weaving two wholly different national cloths.

Canada's history resounds with the recurring struggle between the French and English, from early settlement and colonization in the 1600's and 1700's to the Quebec separatist movement and the election there of the Parti Québécois in 1976. To this day that country struggles to accommodate two languages, two primary identities, within itself. Canada's history has also been deeply affected by its relationship with its southern neighbor, the United States, where a powerful continental

Time Line of Canadian History

Around 13,000 B.C. First Asians cross into North America.

Around A.D. 1000 Vikings arrive in "Vinland," very likely to have been Newfoundland.

1497 John Cabot lands on east coast of Canada.

1534 Jacques Cartier discovers the Gulf of St. Lawrence.

1608 Champlain establishes Quebec City on Indian site.

1642 French settlers found Montreal.

1689–1763 In a series of wars, ending with the final battles known in the United States as the French and Indian Wars and in Europe as the Seven Years War, the British capture Quebec and defeat New France. The Treaty of Paris in 1763 turns Canada over to Great Britain and France retains the islands of St. Pierre and Miquelon just off Newfoundland, territory it holds to this day.

1774 The Quebec Act grants political and religious rights to French Canadians.

1775–1783 During the American Revolution, colonial troops make unsuccessful raids into Canada.

1791 The old province of Quebec is divided into Upper Canada and Lower Canada.

1837–1838 Two short-lived rebellions break out against the government in Upper and Lower Canada. Louis J. Papineau in Lower Canada and William Lyon Mackenzie in Upper Canada lead separate bids for independence. The British, taken by surprise, dispatch Lord Durham from London to study the problems and suggest solutions.

1839 Lord Durham urges self-government for Canada in his report to Queen Victoria.

1841 Act of Union unites Upper and Lower Canada under one governor and legislature.

1867 British North America Act in Great Britain's Parliament creates the Dominion of Canada with four provinces—Ontario, Quebec, Nova Scotia, and New Brunswick.

1869–1870 Louis Riel leads a *métis* rebellion on the Canadian prairies.

1870 Manitoba becomes a province.

1871 British Columbia becomes a province.

1873 Prince Edward Island becomes a province.

1885 Louis Riel leads a second *métis* rebellion on the prairies. The transcontinental railroad, the Canadian Pacific, promised in 1871 as a condition of British Columbia's entry into Canada, is completed on November 7.

1905 Alberta and Saskatchewan become provinces.

1926 A constitutional crisis develops over the right of the governor-general, appointed by the King as his official representative in Canada, to act independently of the elected prime minister.

1939–1945 Canada enters the Second World War and sends forces to serve around the world.

1949 Newfoundland becomes the tenth province.

1954–1959 Canada and the United States build the St. Lawrence Seaway.

1962 The Trans-Canada Highway (the first continuous road across Canada), from St. John's, Newfoundland, to Victoria, British Columbia, is completed.

1965 At age 98 Canada adopts a red-and-white design incorporating a maple leaf as its own official flag.

1967 Canadians celebrate their 100th birthday.

1969 Canada's Parliament passes the Official Languages Act, making the country officially bilingual and requiring the federal government to provide all services in both French and English.

1970 The "FLQ Crisis."

1976 The Parti Québécois, lead by René Lévesque, wins election to run the provincial government in Quebec on a platform promising to seek separation from Canada.

1980 Quebec holds a referendum on "sovereignty-association," the Parti Québécois's initial proposal to separate politically from Canada but retain close economic ties. Prime Minister Pierre Trudeau, himself a Québécois, leads the federal fight against the proposal, which is defeated, 60 percent to 40 percent, so the actual split is not negotiated.

1981 On November 5, after decades of debate, the federal government and all provinces except Quebec reach agreement on bringing Canada's Constitution home from the British Parliament.

1982 Patriation officially occurs on April 17 in Ottawa as Queen Elizabeth II officially proclaims Canada's own Constitution.

1983 Jeanne Sauvé, a member of Parliament, becomes the first woman to be appointed governor-general of Canada.

1985 After nearly a decade in provincial power the Parti Québécois is defeated by the Liberals in Quebec.

1987 After hard bargaining, Prime Minister Brian Mulroney and the ten provincial premiers agree on major amendments to the Constitution in an agreement known as the Meech Lake Accord. In exchange for accepting the Constitution, Quebec receives official recognition as "a distinct society," a controversial step that threatens the unanimous ratification required by all provinces.

1989 After long negotiations, ratification by the U.S. Senate and Canada's Parliament, and a bitter national election campaign in Canada, the Canada-United States Free Trade Agreement takes effect, promising to end virtually all tariffs and customs duties between the two nations and tightening even further what has become the largest economic relationship in the world between two countries.

1990 Under attack from natives, feminists, and others wanting similar special constitutional recognition, the Meech Lake Accord dies two provinces short of unanimous ratification.

But the hotly debated issue does not die, giving rise to renewed (and regular) concern that a successful, confident Quebec will drift off eventually into a separation from Canada. However, in contrast to past incidents, this time polls show large numbers of English-speaking Canadians unconcerned with this once-horrifying prospect.

vision held sway from that rowdy land's quest for independence (and the Continental Congress's formal invitation to Canada to bring its people into an American union) to the Americans' expansionist acquisitions in the nineteenth century.

Vikings

The first Europeans to reach North American shores were the Vikings, who are credited with establishing a settlement possibly at L'Anse aux Meadows in northern Newfoundland around A.D. 1000, nearly 500 years before Christopher Columbus arrived in the Caribbean. L'Anse aux Meadows was not unearthed until the 1960's, when the remains of

Secondary Newcomers

From the east, likely long before Christopher Columbus reached the Caribbean, came the Norsemen, adventurous seamen who, according to one theory, survived North Atlantic storms to set foot somewhere in Canada's far north. Now, two academic colleagues from the University of Manitoba, H. Leonard Sawatzky, a geographer, and Waldemar H. Lehn, a computer expert, are using childhood reminiscences, Canadian geography, computers, and translations of ancient Norse legends to amass evidence that the historic "discovery" may actually have been a series of island-hopping voyages by Norsemen following an Arctic mirage, a visual phenomenon of Canada's north that enables travelers to "see" beyond the horizon.

Arctic mirages differ from their desert cousins in that they reflect something that actually exists, although not where it seems to be.

house sites including a smithy, four boat sheds, and other Norse artifacts were found and carbon-dated. The spot, pronounced "Lancy Meadows" by today's Newfoundlanders, was declared a World Heritage Site by the United Nations in 1978.

European explorers seeking a sea passage to the Far East did not come upon North America until the Age of Discovery in the fifteenth and sixteenth centuries. They called it the New World (and, in turn, Canada's latter-day immigrants typically referred to their homelands as the "old country"). It was these discoveries that launched the struggle for Canada between France and England. The first to lay claim to its shores was Great Britain in 1497, when Giovanni Caboto (John Cabot) landed on Newfoundland or Cape Breton Island (historians are unsure which).

For example, a driver in the desert "sees" a lake ahead that does not, in fact, exist. But under certain conditions a child on a wintry walk to school on the Canadian prairies can see on the distant horizon recognizable buildings of a town forty miles away, far beyond the curved horizon that limits normal vision.

Arctic temperatures can bend light rays around the earth's curve, placing a real image on an elevated, seemingly real horizon. Sawatzky and Lehn believe that the Norsemen saw these real reflections on the Atlantic horizon, leading them ever westward from island to island across the ocean until they ran into northern North America.

Beyond its historical interest, of course, this misleading physical phenomenon carries great import for modern-day travelers such as Arctic fliers, who might be fooled into landing on a runway that is not where it appears to be.

The French: Cartier and Champlain

It was Jacques Cartier, sailing for France in 1534, who led the first real European exploration, discovering the Gulf of St. Lawrence and raising a cross on the Gaspé Peninsula.

Cartier's expeditions gave France its claim to Canada and led to the first tentative settlements, but it was Samuel de Champlain who established the first successful permanent settlement in 1608 at Quebec City. Until his death in 1635, he framed much of the new French colony, exploring and organizing it politically, and came to be known as the father of New France. He was the first European to discover the large lake now named for him, and he explored deep into the North American interior as far as Georgian Bay.

Canada

It was one of those typical Canadian autumn days—windy and brisk despite a strong sun, foretelling the wan winter weeks ahead—when more than 450 years ago Jacques Cartier first sailed up a river that one day would be called the St. Lawrence. By the immense size of the body of water—in fact, by everything about the place—Cartier thought it was a bay, with one side barely visible on the distant horizon from the other.

Like all the initial explorers of Canada, Cartier was on his way to somewhere else. He was seeking the fabled Northwest Passage, the water route around the bothersome top of North America to the equally fabled riches of the Orient. King Francis I of France was seeking a place for new settlements, a place to find new treasures, and new sailing routes to match the New Spain that his European neighbor was carving from the southern New World.

So Cartier continued through the thick fogs, past the dangerous rocks, and into the broad bay at the mouth of the river he would later name for St. Lawrence, the third-century Christian saint. In 1534 he erected a thirty-foot cross on the Gaspé Peninsula to declare French sovereignty over North America. The next year he returned, sailed past his rapidly weathering cross, and went on

Champlain also began fur trading with the Hurons and the Algonquins, the region's native inhabitants, and then supported these tribes against the Iroquois in a military alliance that prevailed throughout most of New France's history.

Since fur trading was the primary reason for establishing the settle-

farther up the river, hoping it would lead to the open sea. Instead, it got narrower and narrower, until finally he was blocked by some impressive rapids. It was a spot later to be known as Quebec City, and there the Frenchman went ashore to talk with some Indians.

What does one call this place? Cartier is believed to have asked in French, sweeping his arm across the horizon. When the sign language finally sank in, the local Indians, thinking he meant their town, replied, *"Kanata."* It was not a name. It was the Huron-Iroquois word for "settlement." But Cartier returned to France anyway to announce his discovery of a new land with a strange, hard name. Thus, conceived in bilingual misunderstanding, did the country get its name forever: Canada.

It was a perfectly symbolic beginning for Canada as a country, misnamed, misunderstood, and mistaken for somewhere else. The country would later have other names suggested: Borealia, Hochelaga, Albionara, Norland, Transatlantia, Superior, and Tuponia. But whatever it was called, it was not India.

The land was rich for sure, but not with diamonds and jewels and spices. And while peacefully conversing, two of the many cultures that would populate the new land were both speaking earnestly and honestly but talking right past each other. There would be many *kanata*s in Canada's history.

ments of New France, the Crown at first was content to let the fur trading companies run the colony. But while the fur trade expanded and Jesuit missionaries arrived to convert the native peoples, the trading companies did not fulfill their agreement with France to bring in settlers. New France desperately needed more inhabitants to buttress itself. Constant attacks by the Iroquois were disrupting the French fur-trading network and increasing the region's vulnerability to pressures from the English.

The English: Frobisher and Hudson

British explorers were already showing their flag and monarch's interest in Canada, adding to the ethnic mix. In their fragile wooden ships Martin Frobisher's crews peeked into the icy void of the Arctic in 1576, 1577, and 1578, leaving five of their members in icy graves after clashes with natives. In 1610 Henry Hudson (sailing for the British rather than the Dutch, who had financed his discovery of the Hudson River) pushed west through the ice until a mutinous crew, fearful of continuing farther into the depths of Canada's harsh elements, set him adrift to perish in the vast bay that later carried his name.

By 1663 when France's King Louis XIV made New France a crown colony and sent regular troops to defend the region, England had gained settlements along the east coast and established successful colonies to the south and east in New England, New York (finally supplanting the Dutch by 1667), Pennsylvania, Maryland, and Virginia. The New Jersey and Delaware regions and large areas to the south of Virginia also were under British control. By 1670, Britain had made an end run around New France and gained the vast lands claimed by the merchants of the Hudson's Bay Company, whose royal charter gave those fur traders control over all the land that drained into Hudson Bay.

French territory in the New World, however, remained far from meager. At its peak in 1712, French possessions covered nearly three quarters of the continent. They stretched from the Gulf of St. Lawrence to Lakes Superior and Huron and included Newfoundland, Acadia (now New Brunswick and Nova Scotia), and the Mississippi River Valley as far south as the Gulf of Mexico.

Within all that New France territory there were only about 3,000 European settlers when it became a colony. Still, a system of government was installed headed by a governor, who was the king's representative and responsible for defense; an intendant, who was in charge of industry, trade, and administration; and a bishop, who was in charge of religious matters including education. This uniquely French system remained intact throughout New France's history and became the grounds for major disputes when the colony came under English rule.

Empires Clash

The struggle for global supremacy saw the French and English engage in a series of struggles over Acadia on the Atlantic coast and over the fur-rich lands of the Ohio and St. Lawrence River valleys. In 1689, after England's King William III entered the War of the League of Augsburg against France in Europe, the French led Indian attacks on New England and New York in North America. The Indians, though allied with the French, had their own goals of defending their land and halting the advance of English settlers. The English retaliated and for a time held Port Royal, Nova Scotia, and attacked Quebec.

The Treaty of Ryswick in 1697 forced both sides to return to their original holdings, but their rivalry remained unchecked. From 1701 to 1713 the War of the Spanish Succession pitted England against France and Spain. While the British failed to capture the fortress city of Quebec then, they succeeded at the treaty table. Under the Treaty of Utrecht in 1713, France relinquished its claims to Nova Scotia, Newfoundland, and the Hudson Bay area but kept Cape Breton Island off Nova Scotia.

For the next thirty years, there was relative peace for New France. Its mighty fortress of Louisbourg on Cape Breton Island was built to guard the Gulf of St. Lawrence and to protect French fishing interests. A chain of forts linking Louisiana with Quebec had also been built, though the links were tenuous because military expenditures were great and the population still relatively small. By 1760, the white population of New France had grown to about 60,000. But by comparison, in that same year the European and African populations of the thirteen British colonies in what became the United States had grown to 1,600,000. The English civilian population in what was to become Canada was much smaller.

When the War of Austrian Succession broke out in Europe in 1744, with the French and English again on opposing sides, the French fort at Louisbourg was a natural target for English in the colonies. Some 4,000 militiamen, assisted by an English fleet under Sir Peter Warren, attacked the fortress and, after a six-week siege, won its surrender in June 1745. That same year French forces reached into New York, burning Saratoga and attacking Albany. The French even got Louisbourg back when the Treaty of Aix-la-Chapelle reinstated prewar holdings in 1748.

No sooner had the treaty been signed than France and Britain again began to prepare for renewed fighting. In 1749 the British built a military and naval base in Halifax, close to Canada's rich forests for decking and masts, and threatening Louisbourg. Both sides built fortifications and pushed into the Ohio Valley. The French with their powerful Indian allies rekindled the fighting in forest battles and frontier-town attacks in western Pennsylvania. That was the beginning of the French and Indian Wars, what in Europe is known as the Seven Years War.

Wolfe and Montcalm
Initially France had the upper hand, but Britain's superior naval strength hindered the French from supplying the colony. In 1758 Louisbourg fell again to the British. One year later the British defeated the French on the Plains of Abraham in the Battle of Quebec. Both General James Wolfe, who led the British, and

the Marquis de Montcalm, who led the French, were killed in this bloody battle. The French governor surrendered the colony in 1760 after three British armies surrounded Montreal. A final reckoning came in the resulting Treaty of Paris in 1763.

English Canada

The British moved to impose anglicization on the former French colony. A royal proclamation was issued promoting the Church of England and

The Treaty of Paris

In 1763, encouraged by the Pope, Britain, France, and Spain signed the Treaty of Paris. Under its provisions much of the final shape of North America emerged: The British got all of Canada and all of France's possessions east of the Mississippi River. Britain also received Florida from Spain. Spain got much of France's territory west of the Mississippi plus New Orleans. And France kept only two little islands in the Gulf of St. Lawrence as unfortified fishing outposts, St. Pierre and Miquelon, tiny, wave-tossed enclaves of French territories that remain today in French hands.

France's defeat suddenly made Britain the most powerful colonial force in North America. The defeat also gave France one more good reason to lend crucial support to the struggling rebels of George Washington in Britain's other North American colonies. These European power struggles in North America prompted the first American administrations to adopt one firm foreign-policy plank: noninvolvement in affairs outside this continent.

the establishment of Protestant schools, and eventually ordering the election of a new assembly, which never met. Since no Roman Catholic could hold office under British law, it meant that a few hundred Englishmen would control the lives of some 60,000 French Canadians. (Britain's previous attempt at anglicization of a French territory resulted in the expulsion of the Acadians from Nova Scotia in 1755, which later prompted Henry Wadsworth Longfellow to write his epic poem "Evangeline," a sad tale of separated lovers whose North American French society was transplanted to Louisiana and became French-speaking Cajun.)

But this time the governor of Quebec, General James Murray, believed that winning the loyalty of the French inhabitants was important. He and his successor, Sir Guy Carleton, refused to call an assembly and asked the government in London to replace the proclamation with more liberal laws, allowing French-Canadian participation. The result was the Quebec Act of 1774, which guaranteed religious freedom and the French system of civil law. It also expanded the colony to include the fertile Ohio Valley. But in so doing, the British fanned the flames of resentment in the Thirteen Colonies.

Loyalists and Revolutionaries

During America's Revolutionary War era, the Continental Congress tried to win support for its cause in Quebec and Nova Scotia. But for most French Canadians it was a conflict between Britain and British colonies. The largest impact on Canada from the American Revolution was the tremendous influx of people into Quebec and what are now the Atlantic provinces by those colonists who wanted to maintain their loyalty to the British throne. Indians, who had been allied with the English, now faced the unbridled threat of expansive colonists with the double burden of having fought against them in the war.

A nineteenth-century print of an original "habitant" of Quebec. National Archives of Canada/Negative no. C 17937

More than 30,000 Loyalists swarmed into the Atlantic region. As a result, in 1784, the colony of New Brunswick was created. Another 10,000 refugees from the American Revolution settled near the Great Lakes and along the northern bank of the St. Lawrence. This led to the division of Quebec in 1791: the western part of the colony, what now includes southern Ontario, became Upper Canada (so named for its position near the source of the northward-flowing St. Lawrence River) and the remainder was known as Lower Canada. Both had assemblies, but the institutions and civil code of the former French regime survived only in the lower province.

Fur Trade

During this time of change, fur trading remained an important aspect of life in British North America. A Montreal-based firm, the North West Company, emerged in 1784 to rival the powerful Hudson's Bay Company. This competition led to new explorations of the west. In 1789, Alexander Mackenzie, a partner in the North West Company, explored to the Beaufort Sea and the mouth of the massive far northern river that now bears his name. By 1793, long before Lewis and Clark, he had even reached the Pacific Ocean by way of the Fraser and Bella Coola rivers. Two other North West employees, Simon Fraser and David Thompson, also led in explorations of the Pacific Northwest; Fraser discovered the river now named for him, and Thompson explored the Columbia River region to the Pacific coast in 1811.

Fur trading also was a source of continuing friction between Britain and the new United States. Although the British had surrendered posts in the Ohio Valley, the Americans complained that the British were arming Indians in the region. Such complaints, along with British interference with American shipping, led to the War of 1812.

War of 1812

In the first year of that conflict, the Americans, expecting Canadian sympathizers to flock to their cause, crossed the Detroit River to invade Canada. Instead, finding no comfort or aid, they retreated to Detroit but were chased by the British and their Indian allies and forced to surrender. In 1813 the Americans successfully raided Fort York, now called Toronto. From Halifax, the British launched their retaliatory attack on Washington, burning government buildings including the White House.

Other battles washed back and forth in the Niagara region not far

The United States *captures the British ship the* Macedonian *in a naval battle near the Madeira Islands during the War of 1812. British and Canadian forces were more successful on land.* National Archives of Canada/Negative no. C 4847

from Buffalo as opposing forces struggled to control the Great Lakes waterways. One of them gave rise to the story of Laura Secord, Canada's Paul Revere, who dressed as a milkmaid to make her way through American lines and warn the British that the Yanks were coming.

The war, however, reached a military impasse. And British and American negotiators signed the Treaty of Ghent in December 1814, ending the war.

Canadian Nationalism   Britain then took steps to strengthen its Canadian colonies by assisting immigration. From 1815 to 1855 about one million Britons arrived. But with the increased population came the seeds of dissatisfaction with the political institutions of the Canadian colonies. While there were elected assemblies, their powers were limited. And ordinary citizens often found their political will frustrated by the powers of appointed officials.

In Lower Canada, where cultural and linguistic biases by both French and English added to the tensions, Louis Joseph Papineau lead a poorly organized and ill-fated rebellion in 1837. In Upper Canada, a reform movement gained a majority in the assembly but was stymied by the appointed Legislative Council. A newspaper editor and assembly member, William Lyon Mackenzie, lead an unsuccessful revolt.

In its wake the British government dispatched Lord Durham to investigate. In his report of 1839, he made two major recommendations: First he proposed uniting Upper and Lower Canada, and second he proposed granting responsible self-government.

Union

With the 1841 Act of Union, Upper and Lower Canada were brought together under one legislature. It became, however, a political nightmare with no single party able to gain enough support from both English- and French-speaking voters to gain a majority in the new legislature.

Pressure mounted. Britain had adopted free trade in the 1840's, which prompted the Canadians to sign a short-lived reciprocal trade agreement with the United States called the Reciprocity Treaty of 1854. A developing rail system in those years also led to closer relations between Canada and the United States. The outbreak of the American Civil War in 1861 raised military tensions, however. And when the massive Union Army proved victorious, there was considerable fear that the Americans would move north to annex some or all of Britain's remaining North American colonies.

Allowing the government to tax directly was as controversial an issue in the nineteenth century in Canada as it was in the United States. National Archives of Canada/Negative no. C 95468

RIEL'S COUNCILLORS IN 1885.

1. Johnny Sansregret
2. Pierriche Parranteau (a famous buffalo hunter)
3. Pierre Gariepy
4. Phillip Garnot, Secretary
5. Albert Monkman
6. Pierre Vandal
7. Baptiste Vandal
8. Toussaint Lucier (reputed to be the strongest man in the North-West)
9. Maxime Dubois
10. Jimus Short
11. — Touroni
12. Emanuel Champagne

Louis Riel's counselors in 1885, with some interesting contemporary observations about two of them. National Archives of Canada/Negative no. C 06688

In 1864 John A. Macdonald, George Brown, and George Etienne Cartier formed a coalition to seek a union of all the Canadian colonies. While Newfoundland and Prince Edward Island remained outside this agreement initially, Nova Scotia and New Brunswick agreed to enter the proposed federal union with Canada (the former Upper and Lower Canadas). The British North America Act, which created the Dominion of Canada (and separated Quebec and Ontario into two distinct provinces) was passed in London and became law on July 1, 1867.

The new federal government, led by Prime Minister John A. Macdonald (later knighted to become Sir John), bought the huge territory of the Hudson's Bay Company in 1869. This land included most of present-day Manitoba and parts of Saskatchewan, Alberta, and the Northwest Territories.

Rebellion

But this move was greatly opposed by the *métis*, people of mixed European and Indian ancestry, who feared their rights would be ignored. Under the leadership of Louis Riel, the *métis* seized Fort Garry (present-day Winnipeg) on the Red River and set up a provisional government. The list of rights they demanded became the terms for negotiating Manitoba's provincial status in 1870. One year later, the colony of British Columbia became the sixth province of the Dominion after Prime Minister Macdonald promised to build a railway to the Pacific within ten years. Financially hard times led tiny Prince Edward Island to join in 1873.

Riel, who had fled to the United States, led a second *métis* uprising in 1885. It too failed, but this time he was captured and executed. For many French Canadians he became a symbol of the effort to restrict French and Catholic rights outside Quebec.

In 1896 the first French-Canadian prime minister was elected. Wilfrid Laurier eased cultural and religious tensions by framing a compromise to the problem of separate schools for French-speaking and Roman Catholic groups in Manitoba, which created a single school system but allowed instruction on religion and in French where student numbers warranted. During his administration immigration from central and eastern Europe was encouraged, so by 1905 Alberta and Saskatchewan had populations sufficiently large to become provinces. But Laurier's plans to build a navy and work out a free trade agreement with the United States cost him the election in 1911.

Canada's War?

When Britain declared war on Germany in 1914, Canada, as part of the British Empire, immediately was drawn into the conflict. Initially there

Prime Ministers of Canada

Prime Minister	Party	Term
Sir John A. Macdonald	Conservative	July 1867–Nov. 1873
Alexander Mackenzie	Liberal	Nov. 1873–Oct. 1878
Sir John A. Macdonald	Conservative	Oct. 1878–June 1891
Sir John Abbott	Conservative	June 1891–Nov. 1892
Sir John Thompson	Conservative	Dec. 1892–Dec. 1894
Sir Mackenzie Bowell	Conservative	Dec. 1894–April 1896
Sir Charles Tupper	Conservative	May 1896–July 1896
Sir Wilfrid Laurier	Liberal	July 1896–Oct. 1911
Sir Robert Borden	Conservative/ Unionist	Oct. 1911–Oct. 1917
	(Wartime coalition)	Oct. 1917–July 1920
Arthur Meighen	Unionist (Wartime coalition)	July 1920–Dec. 1921
(William Lyon) Mackenzie King	Liberal	Dec. 1921–June 1926
Arthur Meighen	Conservative	June–Sept. 1926
(William Lyon) Mackenzie King	Liberal	Sept. 1926–Aug. 1930
Richard B. Bennett	Conservative	Aug. 1930–Oct. 1935
(William Lyon) Mackenzie King	Liberal	Oct. 1935–Nov. 1948
Louis St. Laurent	Liberal	Nov. 1948–June 1957

Prime Minister	Party	Term
John G. Diefenbaker	Progressive Conservative	June 1957–April 1963
Lester Bowles Pearson	Liberal	April 1963–April 1968
Pierre Elliott Trudeau	Liberal	April 1968–June 1979
(Charles) Joseph Clark	Progressive Conservative	June 1979–March 1980
Pierre Elliott Trudeau	Liberal	March 1980–June 1984
John N. Turner	Liberal	June–Sept. 1984
(Martin) Brian Mulroney	Progressive Conservative	Sept. 1984–

was much support for the war effort—volunteer recruitment was high, as were sales of war bonds. But the number of volunteers could not keep pace with the casualty tolls.

Conservative Prime Minister Robert Borden took the issue of military conscription, or the draft, to the electorate in 1917, creating one of the most bitterly fought elections in Canadian history. In Quebec, it was felt that Canada had done enough. Borden's supporters, mainly English-speaking Canadians, called the French Canadians traitors. Military conscription created another long-standing division between Quebec, where antidraft people demonstrated in the streets, and the rest of Canada. Borden won the election in every province except for Quebec, where he was overwhelmingly defeated in an anticonservative vote whose legacy would last for decades.

In the postwar period Canada began taking a separate role in international affairs. It had a seat at the Versailles Peace Conference and became a member of the League of Nations. Domestically, the government took control of five financially troubled railroads and, in 1919, created the Canadian National Railway.

Strike!

Unionism was also taking a strong hold in the west and in Nova Scotia. A radical attempt to create one large union to bargain for all workers led to the Winnipeg general strike of 1919, a year that saw considerable labor conflict in the United States as well. Workers in Winnipeg were attempting to win the right to collective bargaining, but opponents called it a communist conspiracy. The six-week strike ended with its leaders being arrested and the federal government sending in the Royal Canadian Mounted Police to restore order. The resulting violence and deaths not only hurt the government's public image but greatly hindered the growth of unionism in Canada for many years.

An Equal Partner

With the election in 1921, the Liberals took control of the government and William Lyon Mackenzie King became prime minister. Through his efforts and insistence on autonomy in foreign affairs, Britain agreed to the concept of equal status for dominions of its empire. This resulted in Canada's opening its first embassy—in Washington—in 1927.

In 1929 the stock market crashed in the United States, precipitating a collapse of financial markets worldwide. The next decade, the Great Depression, was particularly difficult for Canada. Fully one third of its gross national product involved exports, and with the economies of its trading partners in collapse, there was no healthy market for Canada's natural resources and manufactured goods.

All levels of government came under scrutiny in those difficult years,

The Depression hit hard in Canada.   National Archives of Canada/Negative no. C 20591

Westminster

William Lyon Mackenzie King, grandson of William Lyon
Mackenzie, was leader of the Liberal Party and thus prime minister.
King, fearing a vote of censure from a newly elected Canadian
Parliament in 1926, asked the governor-general to dissolve
Parliament and call new elections. The governor-general refused.
King resigned. A few weeks later his successor, Arthur Meighen,
had his dissolution request granted. King then led a campaign to
gain reelection on the issue of political interference and won a
larger Liberal majority in Parliament. Later that year he joined a
London conference on Britain's relationship with its former colonies.
This produced the Balfour Report, which defined them as
"autonomous communities within the British Empire, equal in
status." In 1931, this was embodied in the Statute of Westminster.

and many Canadians thought it was time for some constitutional
changes to strengthen the federal government. Unemployment was a
provincial concern, for instance, but only the federal government had
the means to deal with such a massive problem in such times. Faced
with similar concerns, the U.S. government expanded its powers and
programs in President Franklin D. Roosevelt's New Deal.

Partners in War

Late in the 1930's, as economies were fueled by preparations for the
approaching war, constitutional changes were moved to a back burner.

On September 10, 1939, Canada declared war on Germany. And while the American government hesitated on its direct wartime involvement until after the Japanese attack on Pearl Harbor, many Americans went to Canada to join its armed forces. Prime Minister Mackenzie King won broad support from Parliament and the public for the war effort by promising a limited overseas role for Canada and no military conscription. But in 1942 King reversed his stand and called for a national ballot on conscription. All the provinces except for Quebec voted for the draft; and once again relations between Quebec and the rest of Canada were strained.

During the war Canada developed closer ties with the United States.

Officers of the 3rd Canadian Infantry Division landing in France on D-Day, June 6, 1944. National Archives of Canada/Negative no. PA 115534

Together, they sent vital supplies by sea to besieged Great Britain. Using only a memorandum of understanding between Canada's prime minister and President Franklin D. Roosevelt, the two countries established a Joint Board on Defense in 1940 to determine the defense requirements of the Atlantic and Pacific coasts in both countries. The Alaska Highway, completed in 1942, was one of its projects, establishing a secure, though long, land route from the continental United States across western Canada to the isolated territory of Alaska.

By late 1942 Canada had five divisions of soldiers overseas from Hong Kong to Italy. In Europe, when the Allies sent 5,000 Canadians on a disastrous commando raid to Dieppe, France, 2,200 were killed or wounded. Canadians played important roles, too, in the Italian campaign, the landing at Normandy, and the liberation of Holland in 1945. Canadians were especially prominent in the air war over Britain and Europe.

Peace and Prosperity

In postwar years Canadians came to enjoy an enormous improvement in their standard of living. New industries, safely removed in North America from wartime bombing, had developed during the war. With new immigration from Europe and a postwar baby boom, Canada's population jumped by 40 percent from 1945 to 1958. Social welfare programs increased, and the federal government often intervened in the economy to assist Canadians, with legislation such as the National Housing Act, which made home mortgages more readily available. Such programs were part of the reason why economically troubled Newfoundland finally joined Canada as the tenth province in 1949.

Prime Minister King's successor, Louis St. Laurent, continued expansion of welfare programs. He is also credited with ending the practice of appealing court cases to the Judicial Committee of the Privy Council in Britain and making Canada's own Supreme Court the final Canadian court of appeal. He and U.S. President Harry Truman also laid the groundwork for the agreement to build the St. Lawrence Seaway, which was completed in the 1950's.

Despite prosperity, the Progressive Conservatives ended the Liberals' twenty-two-year reign of power with the election in 1957, when Conservative John Diefenbaker of Saskatchewan became Canada's first modern prime minister who grew up west of Ontario. He called another election the next year in hopes of winning a commanding majority, which he did—208 of the 265 seats in the House of Commons. The Conservatives continued to expand the social welfare system and, in 1961, introduced a national program of hospital insurance.

Expo '67   The 1960's was a difficult decade for Canada. The economy was lagging, unemployment was high (worsened at times by the arrival of several thousand American draft dodgers and war protestors), and once again French-English tensions increased. Quebeckers (or, as they call themselves, Québecois) increased their demands for special recognition, and small groups of radicals pressed for independence for the province as a separate French-speaking country.

In the 1962 federal election, the Liberals reasserted their control and Lester B. Pearson became prime minister. During his tenure Canadian nationalism grew with the controversial adoption of the maple-leaf flag and the opening in Montreal of the world's fair, Expo, for Canada's centennial celebrations in 1967.

One Nation or Two?

But Pearson was also sensitive to Quebec's growing sense of nationalism, called the Quiet Revolution in that province. He convinced many of Quebec's leaders to participate in federal politics. One of these

At the height of the FLQ crisis a Mountie clashes with a demonstrator in Quebec.
Canapress Photo Service

men was Pierre Elliott Trudeau, who was elected to the House of Commons in 1965, became Justice Minister in 1967, and, after Pearson's retirement the next year, became Liberal leader and prime minister.

In the election of 1968, the unusual and young prime minister's popularity, dubbed "Trudeaumania," carried the Liberals to victory. While Trudeau was associated with Quebec's Quiet Revolution—the silent changes in social expectations and assumption of power by well-educated Quebeckers—he was also a staunch federalist and determined

FLQ

A terrorist organization, the Front de la Libération du Québec, conducted a series of bombings against the ruling English community in that province during the 1960's. Its aim was to achieve separation of Quebec from Canada and end the "Anglo-Saxon colonization" of French Canada.

In October 1970 they kidnapped British Trade Commissioner James Cross and and Quebec Labor Minister Pierre Laporte. Led by Prime Minister Pierre Elliott Trudeau, the federal government, using its powers under the War Measures Act, suspended civil liberties and sent troops into Quebec. On October 17, Mr. Laporte's body was found. On December 3, Mr. Cross was released in exchange for a promise of safe passage to Cuba for the kidnappers and their relatives. Later the same month, the FLQ members were captured and charged with the Laporte murder.

to show that the national capital of Ottawa could promote and protect the rights of French Canadians. Both English and French became the official languages of Canada in 1969 with the Official Languages Act.

During the October Crisis of 1970, when Quebec separatist extremists of the Front de la Libération du Québec (the FLQ) kidnapped British Trade Commissioner James Cross and murdered Quebec Labor Minister Pierre Laporte, Trudeau used his sweeping emergency powers, the War Measures Act, which, in effect, imposed martial law. This was controversial but had fairly widespread support.

But in 1976 the separatist Parti Québecois won the Quebec provincial elections, underscoring Quebeckers' rising ambitions and dissatisfactions with the federal system. This, however, did help to rekindle lagging provincial-federal negotiations over developing Canada's own Constitution. Promising the people of Quebec a "renewed federalism," Trudeau vigorously campaigned against the Parti Québecois's referendum on negotiating "sovereignty association," a new kind of looser association, with Canada. By a three-to-two margin, Quebec voters turned down the proposal while keeping the Parti Québecois in power.

A Constitution at Last

On November 5, 1981, after years of wrangling, Canada's federal government and the premiers of every province except Quebec agreed on a Canadian Constitution and Charter of Rights and Freedoms. And on April 17, 1982, the Canada Act formally went into effect, removing all remaining legislative powers from the British Parliament and placing them in Canada. Although Canada remained a staunch member of the British Commonwealth, the act removed the last vestige of Canada's colonial status.

In 1984 the Progressive Conservatives under Brian Mulroney won the largest federal majority in Canada's history, including most of the

Separatism

Led by René Lévesque, a chain-smoking former broadcaster, the Parti Québecois, or PQ, was an emotional, populist movement of average people that launched a drive to break off Canada's largest province into a separate, at least semi-independent, nation. "Vive Québec Libre" was a popular slogan. It was one thing if the vast, but distant, Northwest Territories wanted to break into two pieces, as that desire emerged in the late 1980's. East and West, each huge but essentially empty chunk would have its own dominant language grouping and its own significant minorities to protect. And some of Canada's English-speaking Anglo-Saxons had had to make some difficult mental adjustments as their country took in immigrants of all different races, religions, and backgrounds.

But it would be quite another thing if Quebec were to drift off into a vague, but separate, limbo. Physically, it would cut Canada in half. And psychologically, it threatened the identity Canadians had constructed in their own minds of a law-abiding, tolerant land that welcomed everyone from turbaned Sikhs to Hong Kong Chinese under each year's quota of immigrants. The thought of a divided Canada was disturbing, too, for Americans, who for so long had taken for granted that their large neighbor to the north would be peaceful and friendly and stable.

Running the Quebec provincial government for four years, the PQ called for a provincial referendum in 1980. Quebec voters would decide on the party's proposal for "sovereignty-association." But the party never fully defined the concept—how much, for instance, it would be separate from Canada with its own set of embassies in foreign countries, its own security forces, its own border guards. Nor did it define how close would be its association with Canada. Would it still use the Canadian dollar as its currency, with the photo of the English Queen on each bill? Would there be tariffs on goods flowing across the Quebec-Ontario border? Prime Minister Pierre Elliott Trudeau, himself a Montreal native, was an outspoken opponent of separatism and an equally outspoken proponent of Quebec's cause within Canada.

After an emotional and hard-fought campaign that saw dozens of Quebec companies and thousands of English speakers flee to another province, over 60 percent of Quebec voters rejected the PQ's plan. Soon after, the party lost political control of the province, although it remained the official opposition party and reorganized for future bids for power.

While many Canadians and American officials breathed a sigh of relief, it would be a mistake to take the vote as an end to Quebec's ambitions. It was a classic Canadian compromise—nothing was finally resolved, but tensions were eased enough so that everyone could get on with ordinary life for a while. However, the subject of Quebec's different culture and its role within Canada would continue to crop up, often over restrictions it put on its English-speaking minority.

In 1987 a different prime minister, Brian Mulroney, who was also a Quebec native, met with the ten provincial premiers to devise a political compact, the Meech Lake Accord. One of the most controversial provisions specified that the new Constitution would always be interpreted with "the recognition that Quebec constitutes within Canada a distinct society." Arguing over exactly what was meant by "distinct society" was the focus of endless debate for years.

While the death of the formal accord in 1990 gave rise to demonstrations and speeches, it changed nothing in actuality. It was but the latest chapter in a long series of estrangements between

Canada's two major language groups with scant possibility of improvement in the future.

seats from Quebec, traditionally a Liberal stronghold. A bilingual Quebec native himself, Mr. Mulroney moved to win finally Quebec's approval of constitutional changes by negotiating a tenuous accord with all provincial premiers acknowledging Quebec as "a distinct society" within Canada, a controversial issue in some English provinces opposed to such entrenched special treatment for Quebec as possibly opening the door to special treatment for Canada's many other distinct parts.

In the end, the agreement collapsed for lack of unanimous ratification by the ten provincial legislatures. And there was across Canada a widespread sense that after more than two centuries the country and Quebec were falling *out* of love with each other. Many English were annoyed with Quebec's moves to limit the use of English there while simultaneously seeking more special recognition for French elsewhere. And the French, increasingly confident with a buoyant economy and free-trade access to large American markets, were angered by rejection of the Meech Lake Accord (named for the Quebec resort where it was negotiated).

In 1988, Mr. Mulroney sought, and won, his party's reelection in a bitter campaign that became, in effect, a referendum on the free-trade treaty that Mr. Mulroney had negotiated with the United States. The treaty, which took effect January 1, 1989, will eventually result in an end to virtually all tariff and nontariff barriers to trade between the world's two largest trading partners. It will, however, likely never bring about an end to Canadian fears of being swallowed, culturally and economically, by their much more populous southern neighbor.

a

Free trade has been a contentious issue in Canada for over a century. The cartoons are from 1891, the photographs from 1987 and 1988. a) Canapress Photo Service b) National Archives of Canada/Negative no. C 95466 c) National Archives of Canada/Negative no. C 6533 d) Canapress Photo Service

b

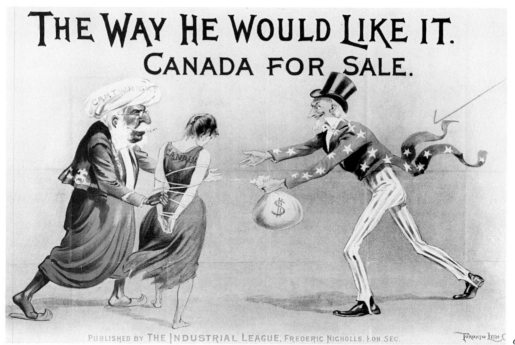

c

d

Many Canadians, One Constitution

The immigration of millions of people has played a large role in shaping Canada's modern personality. Chances are that for the first few generations white settlers came from a British background acknowledging the importance of government, authority, and, of course, the king or queen. The largest early influx to Canada came during and after the American Revolution, when thousands of Loyalists fled by sea and land the emerging democratic rabble of the United States. The descendants of these groups, which saw no point to separating from Britain, remain today as staunchly loyal to the British throne and as a minor conservative influence, much like the Daughters of the American Revolution in the United States.

Scots have long been one of Canada's more powerful minorities, especially in banking and business. Nova Scotia (New Scotland) has summer Scottish festivals and games.   Canadian Office of Tourism

Canadian by Choice or Necessity?

The Loyalists, like virtually all of Canada's later immigrant groups, generally came not because Canada was a challenging new frontier offering an attractive promise for tomorrow, with spices and riches and golden opportunities beyond anyone's imagination. They came simply because Canada was less awful than where they were, an important condition to understanding Canada's conservative national personality. Canada, for instance, was the final destination on the famed Underground Railroad, the secret system of horses, wagons, and sympathetic families in the United States that helped fleeing Southern slaves reach freedom in the years before the Civil War. Britain had abolished slavery in the 1830's at home and in its colonies, so hundreds of American blacks fled to Canada and established several self-contained agricultural communities. It was a path away from trouble to be followed 110 years later by thousands of Americans, black and white, fleeing the military draft for the controversial war in Vietnam.

Later waves of immigrants included a million Americans around the turn of the century who were offered free land in what the Canadian government advertised as "the last best West." In the 1960's Canada, which had long encouraged immigration mainly by white Europeans (and after World War II welcomed Jews), liberalized its entry policies to allow many more immigrants from less-developed countries and from areas such as Africa, Asia, and the Caribbean that brought new interests, themes, foods, cultures, and colors to liven Canadian life. Suddenly, once-staid Canada found the whole character of its population changing until, by the 1980's, one of every eight Canadians had been born in another country. Many did not speak either English or French. And they likely still don't. One survey of Vancouver's public schools revealed that almost half the students had a first language other than English, and of those, two thirds speak mainly Chinese, Italian, or an East Indian language.

These newcomers live in urban ethnic enclaves where they can wear the same old shawls to their ethnic grocery store to speak the same old dialect with friends from across the sea while buying the familiar vegetables to make favorite dishes from the old country. This makes for a continuing delicious ethnic diversity, which is celebrated today in vast week-long city festivals.

Mosaic or Melting Pot?

Canada's carefully preserved ethnic diversity is one of its major differences with the United States. Until recent years the United States has

The Festival of the Autumn Moon in Chinatown, Montreal.   Canapress Photo Service

Two college students in Quebec offer to wash cars. Jennifer Erwitt, *A Day in the Life of Canada.*

believed it believes in the great melting pot where many influences come together. Each makes its own contribution to the larger whole, adds another pinch of spice to affect the national character.

But Canadians believe they believe more in a mosaic of separate pieces, with each chunk becoming part of the whole physically but retaining its own separate identity, color, and tastes. This certainly makes for an interesting mix. Importantly, it provides Canadians with an identity peg, one major way to see themselves as different from Americans, as they must. And as they are.

But when combined with Canada's spread, this mix makes for considerable difficulty in governing. It results in much decentralization and a weak federal system, with provinces wielding considerable political power and always pushing for more. With the provincial pieces squabbling over parochial interests, little concern has been given to the national whole.

French Canada

The most obvious example within Canada has been Quebec. With official encouragement and even legislation, the people and their politicians have clung to their separate ethnic identity with a tenacity that spans almost three centuries and has made them one quarter of Canada's population.

French-speaking Quebec has for many decades been both what made Canada special as a country and what constantly threatened to make it impossible. Virtually no large countries in history have been able to survive intact when they have remained divided by fundamental language differences. Switzerland, with its French, German, and Italian linguistic minorities, is a small country, as is Belgium, where even after many decades French and Flemish-speaking portions regularly confront each other in heated verbal, and many times physical, confrontations. Some of the Soviet Union's many language groups have begun to agitate for more freedoms and even independence, so important has language been to a group's cultural identity.

For two centuries now, French culture has been protected as a separate grouping within Canada. But this did little to change the separatist and often bigoted thinking of either English speakers or French speakers. There could be rampant discrimination on the basis of language on either side. In the late 1960's Canada tried again to safely entrench language rights. The government passed an Official Languages Act, which guaranteed both groups the right to federal services in their own languages. This meant, ideally, that postal tellers, airport workers, government bureaucrats, and others regularly in contact with the public would be equipped to converse with a citizen in whichever language he or she chose. Gradually, this spread to include even everyday items like cereal boxes, which have a French name, contents, and games or offerings on one side and a parallel set in English on the other.

While a significant minority in each language group remained sullen and closed-minded about the other and there have been occasional outbursts of violence, this kind of solution appealed to at least a Canadian ideal of fair play, compromise, and idealism—that Canada would be the first large land to forge a friendly relationship between its two major linguistic groups.

Although only a minority, or perhaps because it was such a visible and audible minority in English-speaking North America, the culture of French-speaking Quebec is possibly the most vibrant. Its music, cuisine, art, drama, and literature sprout naturally and speak to the hopes and needs of Quebeckers that remain foreign to English-speaking Canadians. This is as unchanged today as it was in 1837 when Lord Durham, the British statesman dispatched to report on that quarrelsome colony, reported: "I found two nations warring within the bosom of a single state; I found a struggle, not of principles, but of races." To this

Street musicians perform in front of the entrance to the cable tramway in Montreal.
George S. Zimbel

day Canada's linguistic minorities still quarrel over the rights of each. And French Canadians recall the Quebec humiliation and discrimination with a potent little slogan that adorns every single Quebec license plate: *Je me souviens* ("I remember").

A Taste of Canada

Tourtiere, or pork pie, is a traditional Canadian food favorite from Quebec, especially popular on brisk, autumn days when the light is getting shorter and the winds stronger. Here's how to make it:

Start with two pounds of pork butt, trimmed and chopped fine.
Crush 1 clove of garlic and add.
Peel and finely chop 1 medium onion and add.
Add ½ cup water.
Add ¼ teaspoon of celery salt and another ¼ teaspoon of ground cloves.
Mix thoroughly with salt and ground pepper to taste in a saucepan and let simmer until tender, usually about 20 minutes. Then stir in ¼ cup of dry bread crumbs and let cool.
Now make a double 9-inch pastry pie shell. Roll out one layer of pastry on a floured surface and line a 9-inch pie pan with it. Then cover the pastry with the pork filling. Roll the remaining layer of dough, cut a small vent hole in the middle, and then cover the pork filling, crimping the two layers of dough together around the edges.
Bake in a 350° F. (175° C.) preheated oven until browned, usually about 35 minutes. Let sit for several minutes before serving. This should provide about four portions.

The Notre Dame Basilica in the Sacred Heart Chapel in Montreal. George S. Zimbel

Life Beneath Canada

One day not too many years ago Reggie Bouffard came home from school in his Quebec town to learn a painful lesson about the natural-resource business. His father had died somewhere around the 1,000-foot level of the asbestos mine down the street in Thetford Mines. A rock the size of a truck had fallen from the ceiling. A few days later a teenaged Mr. Bouffard dutifully honored the request of his impoverished mother. He left school and went to work in the mines for the money.

There are thousands of men like Mr. Bouffard who have spent most of their lives pulling things from the ground for employers in distant places. Ever since the nineteenth century, when residents of northeastern Quebec found the fuzzy fibers in the ground and began weaving them into clothing, asbestos has been the economic focus in Thetford (pronounced TET-ford), a community of 28,595, where 27,879 speak French and just about everyone has something to do with the mines that underlie the entire area.

They work long hours in the dusty pits and shafts of these mines, blasting the rock loose, carrying it, crushing it, and hauling the refuse and pebbles to human-made mountain ranges of tailings that sprawl across the landscape. They sort the little asbestos fibers into ninety-five grades, bag them, and load them onto trucks and ships bound for foreign sites. The work brings upward of $700 million a year into Canada.

There are strikes sometimes, and promotions and raises and weddings and births and deaths. Some men try, halfheartedly, to break away and find work elsewhere. But relatives send them local newspaper want ads, and if there is the slightest possibility of a job "back home," the men and their lonesome wives will rush back.

Some of the men die violently underground. Some die in their beds years later, complaining of the severely short breath that everyone just associated with old age until distant doctors diagnosed a new fatal disease called asbestosis.

In their youth, young men like Mr. Bouffard could earn about $26 for their forty-eight-hour work weeks underground, where they swung eight-pound sledgehammers until more efficient mechanical stonecrushers came along. Today, they earn over $12 an hour.

Elsewhere in the world there are multimillion-dollar liability lawsuits, asbestos cleanups, and bans on its use in buildings such as schools. The mines are run more cleanly now. Now and then some older friend falls victim to the condition. But something so familiar to so many is hard to see as a villain. "Why are people so afraid of asbestos?" Mr. Bouffard asks. "I was not afraid in the old days. I had no choice to be afraid, you see? You have to earn money to live, no? Maybe you get sick, maybe not. Today you can get afraid of anything. You can get cancer from soup."

The miners and their families look at these deadly diseases the way many American city dwellers view muggings. It happens, though not as often as most of the world imagines. Everyone knows someone it has happened to. But no one believes it will happen to them.

And so the mines still draw the sons who follow their fathers who followed their fathers. When the mines opened back in 1950, they were at the 650-foot level. Today they are mining the 1,200-foot level while crews prepare the 1,500-foot level, following the gray, dusty veins of asbestos that once were formed in volcanoes and now run under the region for 100 miles or more. "If I had a better education, I might have gone elsewhere," adds Mr. Bouffard, who didn't.

Many Solitudes

There are many solitudes across Canada. The Inuit in the eastern Arctic. The Inuit in the western Arctic, one sixteenth of the way around the world. The Indians from above the tree line. The Indians from below the tree line. Full-blood Indians and *métis*. English-speaking Canadians in a French-speaking Quebec. French-speaking Canadians in an English-speaking sea. Germans in Alberta. Ukrainians in Manitoba. Chinese, Pakistanis, and Indians in Vancouver and Toronto. In the 1970's when Prime Minister Pierre Elliott Trudeau, a staunch believer in Canadian unity and a strong federal government, would talk in western Canada about Canada's two peoples, those who spoke English and those who spoke French, he was laughed at. These were the two primary peoples to Mr. Trudeau, who came from Quebec and remained outspoken even after leaving office. But many citizens of Alberta, for instance, had never known any French-speaking Canadians, who are outnumbered there by German-speaking Canadians and Chinese-speaking Canadians. This problem persists as western Canadians resent granting Quebec more special status and not, say, their own Ukrainian enclave. The west's annoyance was increased by the fact that since 1991, its population had exceeded Quebec's.

One Toronto radio station broadcasts in thirty languages, including announcements on arrival delays for flights from "back home." In many Vancouver neighborhoods the street signs are in two languages, English and Chinese. One Toronto television station survived simply by broadcasting programs in many languages aimed at many different ethnic communities, including movies in Urdu with English subtitles. Toronto's city government routinely prepares its annual property tax notices in six languages: English, French, Chinese, Italian, Greek, and Portuguese.

Landed Immigrants　　And the government often helps continue these divisions. There is a special category of legal newcomer in Canada, called Landed Immigrant. This status permits the person to live in Canada as a regular citizen without giving up his or her original nationality. As long ago as the Quebec Act of 1774, the British Parliament entrenched the separation of Canada's two language communities by guaranteeing religious freedom to Roman Catholic French Canadians and by even instituting an entirely separate legal system, French civil law, for French Canadians in Quebec courtrooms. Besides perpetuating parallel societies within one, it also built in substantial government financial aid for parochial schools, which in Canada, appropriately enough, are called Separate Schools. (In the United States, with its constitutional prohibitions against mixing church and state, such direct aid was nonexistent.)

Region Against Region　　These differences are complicated by a strong historical sense of regionalism or localism and a weak allegiance to the larger, ill-defined country. Back in 1907 Henri Bourassa, a prominent politician, lamented, "There is Ontario patriotism, Quebec patriotism, or western patriotism, each based on the hope that it may swallow up the others, but there is no Canadian patriotism." Long before there were demonstrations against the Vietnam War in the United States of the 1960's and 1970's, there were street riots in Canada over World War II military conscription.

Insulated from one another by geography, language, culture, and economic self-interest, Canadians go about their daily business happily affluent in the main but susceptible to constant sniping and regional bickering. Even in professional football Canadians build in divisions not along team lines but regional lines; the Grey Cup, the annual championship game in November, pits not the two best teams in the Canadian

Football League but the best team from the east against the best from the west. Bruce Rankin, one of Canada's most outspoken and experienced ambassadors, got into a lot of political trouble some years ago when he called his fragmented compatriots among the world's most "negative, parochial, and balkanized people." Some Canadians said he should not have said it, but no one disputed his analysis.

National Parties

Another problem undermining national unity has been that there have been no permanently national political parties with firm bases and leaders in all parts of the country. They could have helped define the Canadian identity and Canadian interests, as opposed to regional interests. They could have helped smooth over the inevitable misunderstandings and grievances in a country that large and helped parcel out political and economic compromises to every corner. Instead of national parties, there have been basically two regional parties—the Liberals and the Progressive Conservatives—plus the socialist New Democrats, an ideological minority in Canada, who made infrequent forays into each other's strongholds.

But there are some signs of significant change. In the parliamentary elections of 1984 the Progressive Conservatives of Prime Minister Brian Mulroney won the largest majority in the House of Commons in Canada's history, including most of the seats from Quebec, a traditional Liberal stronghold. Then in 1988, despite a divisive campaign over the free-trade pact between Canada and the United States, Mr. Mulroney's party won another majority. So divided and fickle had Canadian voters been that this was the first time in thirty-five years that any Canadian party had won two consecutive majorities, and the first time in the twentieth century the Conservatives had done it.

Constitutional Compromise

Besides the appearance of some national political allegiances, there were other signs of change and

How Canada Is Governed

Canada is a democracy governed by the parliamentary system of government. There are two houses in the Parliament—the Senate, which has 104 members appointed by the governor-general on the advice of the prime minister, and the Commons, which has 295 members elected by plurality from ridings, or districts, around the country.

There are three parties with members in the Commons—the Progressive Conservatives, the Liberals, and the New Democrats. Each party has a leader elected by party conventions held at irregular intervals. The leader of the party that controls a majority becomes prime minister and the nation's political leader. The prime minister appoints a cabinet from his or her party's parliamentary members. They oversee various departments, such as agriculture and external affairs, and meeting together, they set government policies.

If no party has a majority in the Commons, then the leader of the largest party seeks to negotiate a coalition with another party's leader. Official government terms of office are five years, but a prime minister can call an election anytime, and usually does so during the fourth year, at a time when the leader thinks the governing party will fare best. If the party in power loses an important vote in the Commons, then the prime minister has to call another election. But no one actually votes for prime minister in national elections. He or she is elected from a local district like all the other members and becomes prime minister because party members chose him or her as party chief.

The formal chief of state in Canada is the governor-general, a largely ceremonial office appointed by the queen or king of England and representing the monarch. It is the governor-general who initially welcomes high-ranking foreign dignitaries, signs legislation, and reads the government's formal policy declarations at the opening of Parliament.

Each province and territory, in turn, has its own one-house parliamentary system with members elected from local districts, differing parties, and party leaders. The local leaders become provincial premiers if their party wins a majority in the provincial legislature during elections called according to each province's own political calendar.

growth, too. Among other things, the new Constitution of 1982 established the equality of English and French in all federal institutions and in the legislature and government of New Brunswick, which has a large French-speaking population. The Constitution allows use of French or English in the legislatures or courts of Manitoba or Quebec. It protects the rights to education in English or French of the linguistic minority in any province or territory, and affirms the rights of Canada's aboriginal peoples, the Indians and Inuits. The Canadian Charter of Rights and Freedoms protects the fundamental freedoms, legal rights, and democratic responsibilities of all Canadians. Until 1982, Canadians assumed they possessed these rights of individuals, although these rights were not written down anywhere.

Courts

These laws are enforced by the police and protected by a two-layer court system. Two provinces—Ontario and Quebec—have established their own provincial police. The other eight provinces and both territories have contracted with the federal police force to provide provincial services. In English, this famous force is called the Royal Canadian Mounted Police. In French, it is the Gendarmerie Royal du Canada. Founded in 1873 as the North-West Mounted Police, these plainclothes and uniformed officers are better known in both languages by their initials—the RCMP or the GRC. Since 1975, their ranks also have included women.

The courts are divided into provincial and federal jurisdictions but are considered one system. This applies even though nine provinces and two territories operate under the traditional system of British common law, which relies on precedents or the cumulative history of judges' decisions, while Quebec's courts have adapted to its needs the old French civil code and procedures, which rely on following a set of written rules. Appeals from the highest provincial courts can be made directly to Canada's Supreme Court, which was established in 1875 as the highest criminal and civil court. It consists of nine members, who must retire at the age of seventy-five. But like many institutions within the living compromise that is Canada, Quebec is guaranteed a minimum number of seats, in this case three.

A Judge in the Basement

Justice comes to Grand Centre, Alberta, every Wednesday and sometimes on Friday. His name is Marshall Hopkins.

He is one of sixteen Alberta provincial judges who still ride the circuit just like the old days. Today, the circuit riders no longer travel on horses; they use airplanes or vehicles with tape decks and cruise controls to travel around their assigned territory, or circuit, spending one day in one town, the next in another. They hold court in ice rinks, police stations, and fire halls. They hear cases on everything from narcotics dealing and armed robbery to littering and poorly placed moose-hunting tags.

Alberta's towns and cities go through cycles of boom and bust, depending on the price of oil and the profits in the search for it. New bedroom towns have emerged; three weeks of every month such communities are populated by children and working mothers. One week each month the fathers return to rest and spend money earned on oil rigs as distant as the Arctic and the North Sea. Family life in this pattern often means trouble with juveniles and domestic disputes.

One certain trouble spot is Judge Hopkins's circuit, an area of 5,000 square miles and around 30,000 people centered on Grand Centre. In Alberta a provincial judge is considered to have a full court calendar if he or she presides over 3,500 cases a year. Judge Hopkins regularly handles 6,500 cases, some days holding court for twelve hours and traveling through blizzards of snow and bugs. "Frankly," the six-foot-four-inch judge said as he cruised down a deserted highway to the day's trials, "I love this work, talking to people, listening to them. I can't imagine any job anywhere I'd rather do. Bar none!"

Judge Hopkins is the son of a pioneer who surveyed the area of northeastern Alberta that is now his son's judicial circuit. The judge is the great-great-grandson of a captain in the Welsh Fusiliers who came to Canada to fight the Americans in the War of 1812. They captured him. The British ransomed him back and he stayed in Canada to raise seven sons, four of whom ended up as American cowboys. The judge's mother was a Québecois who spent part of her life in New England whenever the job situation in Canada was bad. His father was a British land surveyor, and the judge grew up thinking that every child naturally spoke English to his father and French to his mother.

Judge Hopkins remembers being poor, going barefoot in the Alberta summers, and watching his father bargain with Indians to buy his family handmade moccasins each autumn. He left as a teenager and spent the first seventeen years of his working life as a Mountie and, then, as an itinerant construction worker in eastern Canada, which western Canadians regard as crowded. But the future judge missed the broad skies of the west and working daily with legal problems. So he studied law on his own, and before the province required a lawyer's exam, he was appointed a provincial judge, where he earned a reputation as stern but understanding.

By eight each morning, Marshall Hopkins, wearing a business suit, western boots, and a parka, begins the two-hour drive to his distant courtroom to become the Honorable Judge Marshall Hopkins of the Provincial Court in and of the Province of Alberta. His courtroom often is rented for $100 a day in a former dance-hall balcony over a coffee shop.

In one typical day he heard forty-four cases, including eight nonjury trials and eighteen matters adjourned until later. He ordered three people arrested for not appearing in court on time. "I'm very tough on respect for the courts," said the judge. "When that goes, so does the whole fabric of society."

Fourteen defendants pleaded guilty and were fined more than $1,600 in total, the majority for alcohol-related offenses. Aware of the tape recorder recording all the proceedings, Judge Hopkins runs the courtroom briskly and firmly. "The next time I see you here for drinking too much," he told one offender, "you've got four months in the slammer, and if that doesn't motivate you, tough." Perhaps remembering his own four children, including an adopted Indian teenager, and his own teenage brush with the law when an understanding Mountie steered him straight to a firm father's painful spanking, Judge Hopkins is more fatherly with juveniles. He offers first offenders advice and probation instead of punishment. "Eighty-five percent of these kids we'll never see again," he said. "Why make it harder?"

At one point during yet another child-abuse case, he calls a recess to let himself cool down and remember that applying the law is what's important, not his own mounting anger. He is philosophical about the crimes he sees. "I don't get depressed over what people do to each other," he said. "It's disturbing, of course. People don't seem to ask themselves 'What's right?' anymore. They just say, 'How much can I get from this other fellow?' I sit back and observe. Here's man acting out a game. We practice self-deception so much to create an image of humans as so humane while we're denying our animalistic instincts. We're far from perfect, all of us."

Then, by early evening Judge Hopkins is usually headed home in the dark to his wife, Toni, across the snow-covered countryside where the stunning nighttime silences are still broken by a coyote chorus. Wildlife remains a prominent part of the Canadian countryside. Some provincial governments like Alberta's even plant crops on scattered fields and then leave them unharvested to nourish rabbits, herons, ducks, geese, moose, eagles, deer, and weasels, the province's nontaxpaying population.

It is at such pensive times, with the tape music playing softly, the cruise control holding the car right at the legal 62 miles an hour, and his eyes ever alert for wildlife on the highway, that Judge Hopkins ponders some of his own doings. "One day when I was a lot younger," he said, "I saw a coyote in a field far from the road. To scare him, I fired my pistol in the air. And even at that distance, he fell. I went over there, and both his back legs were broken, and I just stood there. I had to put him out of his misery. I was so stupid, you know. Just fooling around and he paid for it. A beautiful animal he was. He had a right to live, too. I've thought about that so many times over the years. I guess we all make mistakes. That's why I'm in business as a judge."

Daily Life

The Average Canadian

The average Canadian is about thirty-four years old, but more than two million are over age sixty-five, a forewarning of the aging population that is putting greater financial strains on the government's many benefit programs. Three out of four Canadians live in cities, two out of three in their own homes (and one out of every seven homes is heated by wood). About four of every ten Canadian marriages will end in divorce (one fifth of them after twenty years). More marriages seem to last in the island province of Newfoundland, while more seem to wane on Canada's other coast in the province of British Columbia.

Canadians are having fewer children, down to 1.7 per woman compared to 3.4 at mid-century. Every tenth mother is under age twenty, accounting for a large part of the 600,000 struggling households with a single parent. In 1945, 1 out of every 20 babies died before its first birthday; today the rate is 1 in every 100, one of the world's best and significantly better than the United States rate.

Canada's diverse regions are also reflected in family sizes, with 4 persons in the average Newfoundland family and 3.3 in British Columbia's average family. And there has been a dramatic movement away from several generations of a family living together, from about 7 percent of all households in 1951 to only 1 percent now.

National Health

Canadians are living better, thanks to the government's expensive national health plan, which pays at least 75 of every health-care dollar, compared with about 43 cents in the United States. As one result, the average Canadian man can now expect to live through a little over 72 hockey seasons, 7 more than a World War II baby and 1.2 years longer than an American male. The average Canadian woman can expect to live until 79, 10.5 years longer than her World War II mother and nearly one year longer than an American woman.

Suicide, Cigarettes, and Drugs   The greatest killer of Canadians at age twenty-five is motor-vehicle accidents, followed by suicides. Number three for men is drowning, and for women strokes. In 1945, more than half of all Canadians did not attend school past the eighth grade. (In Canada, high school often runs through grade 13 and University can be three years.) Today, more than 80 percent of Canadians go through at least the ninth grade, while the number with post-secondary education has climbed from 1 in 30 to 1 in 3, one of the major reasons behind the massive growth in audiences for all aspects of Canadian culture.

· 153 ·

A Symbol of Change

Charles Clark sat in his living room puffing on a pipe and watching the silent street scene outside as the youngsters of High River, Alberta, crunched through the snow that morning on their way to school behind the neat rows of giant fir trees that were not planted yesterday.

High River's first settlers put them in more than ninety years ago. Many of those settlers were Americans, creaking along the old Macleod Trail on wooden wheels from Montana to the government-promised land in Canadian territory. The people of High River liked the trees along their narrow trail then. And they still do today, when the road is still called Macleod Trail but the vehicles are much larger and faster. But only someone from outside High River would ever suggest chopping down the pioneers' legacy of trees to make way for progress.

The tallest point in Quebec towns is always the steeple of a Roman Catholic church. In northern Manitoba the tallest points are the golden domes of the Eastern Orthodox churches. In Saskatchewan and Alberta the tallest human-engineered point is always a grain elevator, those green, red, and gray "prairie cathedrals" that stand by the lonely railroad sidings ready to ship their agricultural bounty out to the world.

Once upon a time these small communities dominated Canadian life. But today cities do; more than three out of every four Canadians live in an urban area where cement and steel, hotels and refineries, dominate the skyline. Left behind in all this change from an agrarian society to an urban one are the sedate, tidy communities such as High River, which have produced the foods and the values for the larger land. In these towns the work is still governed by the seasons. Success seems always to depend on faraway factors and markets. And the penetrating frost still squeezes up a goodly crop of new rocks every spring.

Charles Clark grew up in this older Canada, back when horseback riders were the only travelers and the only road signs were marks on tree trunks.

For years many of these towns flew the flags of both Canada and the United States. Many settlers, including Mr. Clark's wife, Grace, had come from the States. So the towns had two Thanksgivings each year: one in October for northern Canada's earlier harvest and another in November for the Americans marking their Pilgrim heritage and later harvest. There were also two July independence festivals—on the first for Canada and on the fourth for the States.

Everyone worked in or around town. A person's reputation depended on his or her word. Everybody knew everybody. High River was smaller than its current population of 4,000. People would sit on the veranda of a summer evening and talk about the day and work. Much of those details made their way into Mr. Clark's newspaper, the *High River Times.* "We were settled by people who came to stay," said Mr. Clark. "They weren't coming to make a fortune and move on."

The settlers were sturdy, independent stock. On the weekends Mr. Clark and his two sons would go hiking in the bush and they would happen upon homesteading families, scratching out a living from the wilds. They might go to town twice a year to pay bills and buy supplies in stores where harnesses hung from the ceiling and giant homemade cheeses sat on the counter. Communities were built on cooperation; everyone pitched in to help rebuild a neighbor's burned barn. Then the difficult Depression of the 1930's set many families back. "Just when things could have gotten better, and the country take off," said Mr. Clark, "everyone's worst possible fears were fulfilled. It set the country back a long ways."

In those days, he recalled, society's links seemed to run between individuals, not official bodies. "You'd never think of going to a government for aid. You'd do it yourself or go to a neighbor. Today there are always a dozen committees and bodies you've got to go through, and there's always someone opposed. That drains people's independence and initiative. Life is getting all cluttered up with rules and regulations. It's changed the whole character of our society."

Now, he said, people are more concerned with their own interests. "Selfishness has taken over. Youth expects to be handed everything on a platter. Each community, small and large, becomes fragmented by all these competing interests. And you have not got compromise anymore but confrontations all the time. Canada wasn't started by confrontations. You must have compromise and cooperation to build anything new here. But those people in Ottawa are bent on confrontation, and they act so damn busy they don't remember what the real Canada is. The simple times as we knew them are gone forever. And every field has a 'No Trespassing' sign."

For many years the Clarks went about their simple but busy retired life, he doing errands and attending hospital board meetings, she tidying up their house with all the living-room pictures of their sons, their wives, and their children. "We could do with a few more grandchildren," said Mrs. Clark, "but you know, daughters-in-law these days have their minds set on a different career." And Mrs. Clark kept her ear to the radio for all the latest news. "We seem to have so many problems without solutions," she said.

One of their sons, Joe, bought his parents a modern microwave oven, which the couple rarely used. They refused, too, to get a dishwasher. They traveled sometimes, around Canada or even to Europe. But they found they could not do without the familiar, sturdy life in their little High River home back on the Macleod Trail. "I can never understand," said Mr. Clark, "why some people wear themselves to pieces in the city to earn enough money to go back home again where they came from."

The elderly Mr. Clark never really left where he came from. And when it was time to go forever, the old Canadian pioneer died upstairs in the same old bedroom where he had been born. His sons, Joe and Peter, had been born there, too. But when they got the news about their father, Peter was in Calgary, and Joe, once the prime minister of Canada, was in Ottawa, leading their new lives in a modern Canada. And one more piece of Canada's past was gone.

At the end of World War II in 1945 only 24 percent of all Canadian women held jobs outside the home. Today, half do, and two thirds of them are married, although their wages remain smaller than men's for the same work. A typical Canadian worker spends less than 40 hours a week at work and more than 50 hours in leisure-time activities, with 100 percent watching television and 83 percent reading a newspaper or listening to a radio. Talking is also a very popular Canadian pastime; there is one telephone for every 1.7 Canadians, and each person makes an average of 1,000 calls every year. (Christmas records the most phone calls, while Mother's Day is second.)

The average Canadian worker will miss 4.5 days of work each year due to illness, meaning 400,000 out of a total work force of 11 million are absent on any given day. Canadians are big on vacations, too, spending over $6 billion every year. "Vacation travel," said one government study, "is clearly regarded as a necessity by Canadians." They also spend over $8 billion on illegal drugs, and nearly 2 percent of the gross national product goes for beer. Canadians are the world's third-largest

This couple sells roasted chestnuts on Laurier Street in Montreal. The street has excellent shops and restaurants.   George S. Zimbel

soft-drink drinkers (behind only the United States and the leader, Mexico), and the fourth-largest cigarette smokers (behind only Cyprus, Greece, and Turkey). Half of all Canadian children try smoking before they are twelve, but only 40 percent of adults still smoke (versus 28 percent in the United States). Canadians also rank near the top in saving money—about 14 percent of everything they earn, or nearly three times the American savings rate. Today there are 6 million more savings accounts in Canada than there are people.

They are also among the world's less violent people. For a long time Canada has recorded around 600 homicides a year, one third the number killed annually just in New York City. One explanation: In Canada, firearms restrictions are tougher. A gun license requires study and testing just like a driver's license.

Hockey and Other Obsessions

Nearly half of Canada's total population participates in some sport. Park fields are jammed with baseball, volleyball, and soccer players by summer and, in winter, flimsy barricades are put up everywhere and water is sprayed on the ground to form thousands of inexpensive ice rinks. The seventh-inning stretch at many professional baseball games is used for some brief calisthenics, led by enthusiastic young people standing on the dugout roof and followed by just about everyone in the stadium.

Teenagers competing in minor-league hockey.   Doug MacLellan/Hockey Hall of Fame

Traffic on quiet residential streets must weave around the homemade nets erected by youngsters for endless street-hockey games. Children are roused at 4 and 5 A.M. on cold Saturdays because that is the only time their little-league hockey team can find open rink time at the 24-hour arenas. So intense is the interest that some high schools field a half dozen or more varsity-level hockey teams. And when Team Canada is playing the Russians on television, restaurants and bars know they might as well close down, so empty do the streets become.

Hockey is, of course, Canada's national sport. Professional games are the focus of many Saturday nights. Season tickets are handed down in wills like priceless art objects. And minor-league hockey is where ambitious Canadian boys skate and furiously check each other into the boards during weeks-long cross-country campaigns as early as their mid-teens. The teams are followed equally furiously by local residents whose civic identities seem inextricably tied to the fortunes of players, some of whom will become pros. They perfect their skills to the raucous cheers of enthusiastic crowds during countless games separated by endless hours on dark team buses moving through the night on to the next rink while the players try to sleep.

So close and intense is the identification between Canadians and their teams that it became a matter of national concern and debate in 1988 when the Edmonton Oilers traded Wayne Gretzky to the Los Angeles Kings. It was something akin to selling a precious national resource. Canadians can easily understand how 85 percent of the pros in the National Hockey League are Canadians, although many note that the figure is down from 92 percent. This means that Chicago's Blackhawks or Minnesota's North Stars are really teams of Canadians playing for American cities. Of course, the reverse is true in baseball, where Toronto's Blue Jays and Montreal's Expos are really teams of Americans playing for Canadian cities. But Canadians have a hard time under-

Canada's national sport is played on most every flat surface all winter, indoor and out, and on roller skates on summertime streets. Canadians still make up three quarters of all the players in the National Hockey League, a misnomer since it involves two nations (and only part of the United States). Brian Miller/Bennett Studios

standing how hockey can remain the single major professional sport in the United States without a major television network contract.

Three Downs, Rouges, and the Grey Cup   To combat the domination of foreign athletes, the Canadian Football League maintains limits on the number of foreign players each team can field. They are called "imports." This guarantees a minimum number of player positions to Canadians, who, strangely, are not called Canadians but are labeled "nonimports." Canadian football rules are different, too; the fields are wider and longer, skillful kicking can earn more points (a ball kicked past the end line and out of play is called a "rouge" and earns a point), all backs can be in motion, and the offense has only three downs to move 10 yards (though off the field Canada uses the metric system). Competing against the more glamorous and richer National Football League in many border-area TV markets, the CFL has fallen on difficult financial times, although its annual championship game, the Grey Cup, is considered so important that both Canadian television networks are allowed to broadcast it simultaneously.

While the National Football League (like the National Basketball Association) has consciously refrained from granting any major franchises to Canadian cities, its dominating shadow, like that in many areas of everyday life, looms over Canadians in other ways. For many years superior Canadian athletes, among many fields of endeavor, have been able to receive more recognition and remuneration outside the country. A British writer, Anthony Burgess, once pointed out Canadians' peculiar position when he said, "John Kenneth Galbraith and Marshall McLuhan are the two greatest modern Canadians the United States has produced." (The first was a major advisor to and ambassador for American Democratic Presidents and the latter, a professor at the University of Toronto, was a pioneering thinker in the field of communications and television.)

A Winter Carnival canoe race in Quebec City. Quebec Tourism Dept.

Winning and Trying

Until recently, Canada has not prized the kind of intense day-in and day-out competition—boys against the girls, this row against that row, this school against an arch-opponent—that is stressed from the first day of school in other societies where winning is, if not everything, then almost everything. Canadian universities believe students go there for an education and perhaps some athletics, if there is time. So none of them offer any athletic scholarships to promising high school athletes. Those youths are often lured to United States colleges.

Outside of hockey rinks, Canadian parents, schools, and institutions, by and large, have stressed more the have-a-good-time-while-trying-hard attitude, and if you triumph, especially over the Americans, that is good, but you probably won't, so don't despair much. Josef Brabenec

One way to get through the long winter is to invent new sports. This bed race is held at the Winterlude in Ottawa. Government of Canada, ISTC

is a Czechoslovakian émigré coach who arrived in Canada in the late 1970's after constructing a rigorous and successful national tennis program in his homeland, producing players the likes of Martina Navratilova. He had some pointed views about Canadian competition. "Canadian kids in general are spoiled rotten, given too much for little or nothing, so they have no incentive to get out and hustle on the cut-throat international scene. Better to stay home and be top dog against other mediocrities. It's not even a fear of failure. They simply don't want to work that hard. They are content to practice what they know, rather than concentrating on improving weaknesses and adding new skills."*

*Nora McCabe, "Give This Man a Chance and He'll Produce a Champion," *Racquets Canada* (March 1978), p. 21.

In 1947 Canada's Barbara Ann Scott became the first North American ever to win a figure-skating crown. But that was a long time before the 1980's, when Canadians, sometimes assisted by imaginative government support programs that reflected a growing national self-confidence, began winning big-time in international competition. In 1982 Steve Podborski, a Canadian, became the first North American to win the men's World Cup downhill ski championship. In the 1984 Olympics Canada's hockey team became the first to puncture the Americans' dreams of repeating their miraculous Olympic gold medal win of 1980. In the 1988 Winter Olympics, held in Calgary, Elizabeth Manley bumped her American competitor out of second place in women's figure skating. (And in the summer Olympics that year, Ben Johnson, a Jamaican immigrant to Canada, at first thrilled his new countrymen by winning the 100-meter sprint finals and then appalled them by testing positive for illegal drug use.)

A wagon race at one of the many summer rodeos held across western Canada. The most famous is the Calgary Stampede; this is in Morris, Manitoba. Government of Canada, ISTC

What's That Sound?

Canadians have long spoken of their worries of being culturally overwhelmed by the United States, even if it was unintentional. But few Canadians, and even fewer Americans, realize how great a cultural contribution many Canadians have made to the cultural life of larger North America over the years in many fields, even if they are rarely identified as Canadians. Canada's popular music industry has spawned Loverboy, Prism, Neil Young, Rush, Rough Trade, Steppenwolf, and Martha and the Muffins. In country music, there has been Anne Murray, Don Williams, Hank Snow, Gordon Lightfoot. Others have included Paul Anka, Dan Hill, Joni Mitchell, Buffy Sainte-Marie, Murray McLauchlan, Ian and Sylvia, Liona Boyd, the Canadian Brass, Oscar Peterson, Glenn Gould, Maureen Forrester, Teresa Stratas and John Vickers, even Guy Lombardo and Percy Faith.

One of the reasons for the music boom at home and the resulting recognition abroad has been a variety of federal Canadian content regulations, which require at least 30 percent of all musical radio programming be written and/or performed by Canadians. On television programs the figure is 60 percent. This helped create within Canada a domestic market sufficient to support homegrown music makers who no longer must leave their country to be considered a success. Indeed, although their egos and desire for fame and fortune may lead many Canadian artists to seek success on the larger North American stage, many others are satisfied with the income and recognition from their home market. This is especially the case in Quebec's French-language culture, where even the most famous pop singers are virtually unknown in the next-door English-speaking province of Ontario.

Canadians have played major roles in Canadian, American, and sometimes British theater and cinema, from Hume Cronyn to Kate

Nelligan. Canadians have played good guys (Walter Pidgeon, Raymond Burr, Glenn Ford) and bad guys (Christopher Plummer, John Colicos, Arthur Hill), happy guys (Leslie Nielsen, John Candy, Jack Carson, Tom Chong) and sad guys (Ben Blue, Lou Jacobi, and Gene Lockhart as the original film Bob Cratchit in *A Christmas Carol*). There have been Canadian cowboys (Rod Cameron, Lorne Greene) and Indians (the original Tonto, Jay Silverheels, in *The Lone Ranger*, and Chief Dan George), presidents (Raymond Massey, Alexander Knox), and even intergalactic space heroes (William Shatner as Captain Kirk of *Star Trek* fame).

America's Sweetheart and Other Canadians

In the early days of movies, an actress known as America's Sweetheart (Mary Pickford) was really a Canadian, as was Superman's sweetheart (Margot Kidder), Henry VIII's sweetheart (Genevieve Bujold), King Kong's (Fay Wray) and James Bond's forever thwarted admirer, Miss Moneypenny (Lois Maxwell). Moviemakers Jack Warner, Louis B. Mayer, David Cronenberg, and Norman Jewison are all Canadian, as is the National Film Board, a government-subsidized entity that has won many international awards, including Oscars, for its long and short films, especially nature documentaries. In recent years Canadian artists have had particular success producing children's programming for television.

Live from . . .

American television reporters Peter Jennings, Morley Safer, and Robert MacNeil are Canadian, as are TV hosts Art Linkletter of Moose Jaw, Saskatchewan, and Winnipeg's Monty Halparin, better known to daytime viewers as Monty Hall of *Let's Make a Deal*. Alan Thicke of the TV situation comedy *Growing Pains* is Canadian, too. Canadians have made Americans marvel at magic (Doug Henning) and especially

The National Film Board

One indelible imprint has been left on Canada's mind by the National Film Board. Created by the federal government in 1939 as a motion-picture-making endeavor to initiate and promote films "in the national interest" and "to interpret Canada to Canadians and to other countries," the board is now believed to be the world's oldest active government film production agency. With headquarters in Montreal and separate French and English departments, it has nursed into creative life many Canadians in areas such as animation, sound recording, and cinema-verité documentaries, many on the wilds and wildlife.

In the early days the board, known in Canada simply as the N.F.B., opened in a converted sawmill and dispatched squads of projectionists on regular routes like cinematic circuit-riders to hundreds of small communities all across the country. There in gyms, classrooms, and dining rooms Canadians, until then exposed mostly to United States films, could see the wonders of their own land and their own lives through the filmed labors of homegrown talent. The board was a pioneer in making documentary films.

The N.F.B. has produced more than 17,000 films, including more than 6,500 original productions and nearly three dozen feature films, including *The First Emperor* and *Mon Oncle Antoine*. Each year, an estimated one billion people see works produced by the N.F.B.

laugh—mimic Rich Little, David Steinberg, Mort Sahl, Dan Aykroyd, Dave Thomas, Rick Moranis, and Lorne Michaels, a Canadian who is more famous as producer of NBC's long-running *Saturday Night Live*.

Inventions from Basketball to Standard Time

Canadians have been busy inventing, too. In 1891 a Canadian doctor named James Naismith sought a safe, energetic game that would be more interesting to do than boring calisthenics. He came up with a game that had nine players on a side and used as a target a peach basket nailed to a gym balcony railing. But this was too many players and the basket's placement let fans reach in to deflect the ball. First played at YMCA College in Springfield, Massachusetts, basketball has enjoyed its greatest popularity in the United States, where hockey has not been as strong competition for players' attention.

Canadians also invented Pablum (by Toronto's Hospital for Sick Children), insulin (Dr. Frederick Banting and Charles Best), the snowmobile (Bombardier Inc.), the banana split (Alfred J. Russell), the sweet McIntosh apple (John McIntosh himself), the chocolate bar (A.D. Ganong), and Canada Dry, the pale nonalcoholic imitation of champagne that J. J. McLaughlin dreamed up on a turn-of-the-century trip to France. And all of this might make some good questions for the board game of Trivial Pursuit, which was invented in 1979 in a Montreal kitchen by two Canadian journalists, Chris Haney and Scott Abbott.

Boy Meets Girl in Winnipeg

It takes many years for a country to become a nation, for a group of people who happen to live together on a piece of land to develop the kind of shared culture of common stories, images, references, and artifacts that bind peoples together, even across vast distances. It took the United States slightly more than a century to develop these bonds to a point where its authors, fueled by a Revolution and a Civil War, felt safe to stop copying British writers and to develop their own Ameri-

Organizing Time

Until Sandford Fleming and the railroads came along, the world's clocks were in chaos. They were each set according to the sun's estimated position in that town or on that street. Thus, if it was noon in Toronto, most of Montreal's clocks would read 12:25, while clocks in other towns would say 12:08 or 11:58. There were 100 different time zones just in the United States of 1883.

That was fine when travel was by horse, because a few minutes one way or the other didn't matter much in a day-long ride. But as provinces, states, and ultimately the world were tied closer together by faster means of transportation and communication, it meant mass confusion. How could a railroad publish a meaningful schedule for each station when each station had its own time?

Mr. Fleming was a Scottish immigrant to Canada (as was Alexander Graham Bell, who invented the telephone and sign

can style. It has been much the same in Canada.

Many Canadians are looking elsewhere less for artistic inspiration. Hugh MacLennan, one of the novelists who has led Canadian literature into new paths, once described Canadian stories as "Boy meets girl in Winnipeg, and who cares?" Canadians were writing their own version of what already had been written, and read, many times elsewhere. In those days Canadian bookstores maintained separate sections for Canadian books, which the owner could claim helped promote them. But the real message, of course, was that there was real writing from other countries and then there were Canadian efforts over there on the special shelf.

language). Mr. Fleming was a practical and a persuasive man. He divided the entire world into twenty-four time zones, each 15 degrees of longitude wide. Then he led the even harder battle of convincing the world's governments to agree to set all their clocks on the hour at the same moment.

There was much opposition to fooling around with God's time, but with Scottish tenacity and the pressing needs of his railroad employer, the red-bearded Canadian engineer and a supportive scientific community succeeded virtually everywhere. And on November 18, 1883, the globe's many lands simultaneously went onto standard time—except in a few places such as Newfoundland, which to this day insists on setting its clocks one half hour ahead of Atlantic Standard Time. Mr. Fleming, who was knighted by Queen Victoria to become Sir Sandford, went on to considerably easier tasks, like building his country's first transcontinental railroad and even designing Canada's first postage stamp.

But that is changing. "We don't have a British fiction section or an American fiction section," said one bookstore owner. "So why should we have a Canadian section?"

Canadians' attitudes are changing, too, about publicity and promotion, garish activities once associated only with noisy Americans. "Taking out ads in the newspapers to tell people how great you were and other forms of blowing your own horn," *Saturday Night,* a monthly magazine, noted, "were considered if not distasteful at least downright un-Canadian. If Canadians did something they thought they should be proud of, they would wait quietly in the corner for the recognition they felt was due them, and if it didn't come, they accepted the neglect as their birthright."* The magazine went on to note that this had changed and that now such people "are regarded impatiently as relics of the bad old days when being Canadian meant always having to say you were sorry."

Change was even creeping between Canada's English- and French-speaking communities. In 1978 when New Brunswick's Antonine Maillet, an Acadian, won France's prestigious Prix Goncourt, it was the highest international honor ever won by a Canadian author. Yet it was an achievement virtually ignored in Canada's English media. But within four years Roch Carrier, a leading Quebec playwright and novelist, could reminisce: "I remember when my books were first translated [into English]—everybody felt it was a kind of treason, giving my books to the rest of the country. But today everybody wants to be on the other side of the frontier."†

Committees of actors have written innovative dramas to help illuminate a locality, whether it concerns struggles over a coalfield or surviving in an urban ghetto. The big land and humanity's relation to it is a major theme of many writers, including the poet Al Purdy. Rudy Wiebe is an Albertan and a writer who explores area history for the sort of human drama that speaks to a universal experience. His characters are not cardboard good and bad guys. As they view advancing whites, his Indians, for instance, display the same kinds of human frailties as the frightened pioneers themselves. Margaret Atwood's fiction often explores the clash of sexes, for which she sometimes reaps better reviews abroad than at home. Joe Fafard, a sculptor from Saskatchewan, portrays in clay an army of characters from his region's past, but their faces, positions, and actions speak to any viewer.

---

*"Hated the Film; Loved the T-shirt," *Saturday Night,* December 1979, p. 4.
†"A Vision That Transcends Borders," *Maclean's,* May 24, 1982, p. 6.

Publishing Canada   A flock of small publishing houses have sprung up to provide outlets for more writers. Canadian culture is like a northern flower, said Paul Thompson, an innovative Toronto theater director. "It bursts out whenever it can and grows hard and fast with lots of color." His players once transformed ten paintings by Gabriel Dumont, a *méti* rebel in the late 1880's, into a full-length drama. His actors have spent an entire summer living with a rural family to portray country life. "Canadian actors were not using their capacity to observe life around them," added Mr. Thompson. "They were modeling themselves on United States plays and actors. So we build our own plays that strike deeper." Quebec now has more than 300 theater companies employing professional actors. Toronto alone has about four dozen independent theatrical companies. In Calgary, downtown workers clutching their sandwich bags vie for limited seats at lunch-hour theater performances. Many television and film dramas now are filmed in Canada to benefit from the banks of theatrical talent and a currency differential that makes it cheaper to work in the north. Many American plays and movies are first tried out on Canadian audiences. "In Canada," said Mordecai Richler, a Montreal native, a longtime judge for the Book-of-the-Month Club, and author of many works, such as *Joshua Then and Now* and *The Apprenticeship of Duddy Kravitz,* well known south of the border, "there's a tradition evolving at last and it's worth defending. There's more good, honest writing in Canada now than twenty years ago. We should count our blessings."*

Much of that focuses on a deep love for the land and its rhythms, what another Canadian author, Farley Mowat, who wrote *Never Cry Wolf*, calls "the unity of life" on earth. "You destroy any one part of it," he

---

*"Nationalism Hurts Culture, Author Says," *Toronto Star*, October 25, 1978, p. A4.

said, "and you are in a sense destroying part of yourself." So by trying to preserve animals like wolves, he argues, humankind is also trying to save itself. Besides Mr. Mowat, readers in many lands outside Canada have been reading the words of Canadians such as Saul Bellow, Arthur Hailey, Will Durant, Kenneth Millar (better known as mystery writer Ross Macdonald), Alice Munro, and Robertson Davies. "Nations have a way of whispering the inner truth about themselves," says Mr. Davies. "No ghosts in Canada? The country which too vigorously asserts its normality and rationality is like a man who declares that he is without imagination; suddenly the ghosts he has denied may overcome him, and then his imaginative flights make poets stare."

The Group of Seven

If ever there was any question about the impact of Canada's landscape on the minds, thinking, and identity of its people, the enduring works of a school of modern artists known as the Group of Seven will dispel them.

Their raw, skilled depictions of Canada's wilderness, boldly painted and touched with a sense of mysticism, rebelled against the predominant nineteenth-century realism. This new style and their efforts to gain recognition as Canada's national school of painters initially turned the art establishment against them.

While not formally founded until 1920, when they had their first showing as a group at the Art Gallery of Toronto, the original members were J.E.H. MacDonald, Lawren Harris, A.Y. Jackson, Franklin Carmichael, Arthur Lismer, Frederick Horsman Varley, and Franz Johnston. They came to know each other through their work; all but Harris were commercial artists and several even worked for the same company, Grip Ltd., in Toronto. In their early years the group actually included an eighth artist, Tom Thomson. He died in 1917, but his enthusiasm for

Canada's wild north country had a profound influence on the others.

Like many European Postimpressionists, the Group sought to convey a deeper sense of their feelings for subjects in paintings and less of their objective representation. They often painted together in the studio or in the bush country of northern Ontario, and their early works share in a vivid and rich coloring and heavy use of impasto, the thick layering of paint.

Initially, they had many critics, but they found a champion in Eric Brown, director of the National Gallery of Canada. He began buying

The Jack Pine *by Tom Thomson.*   National Gallery of Canada, # 1519, oil on canvas

their works even before they were established as a group, and in 1924 he included their work in Canadian exhibits sent to the highly regarded Wembley exhibition in England. At first this only heightened criticism back home, but that soon faded in the face of favorable reviews in the British press. Supporters at Toronto's Arts and Letters Club and the *Canadian Forum*, a prestigious monthly journal, helped gain them recognition nationally as Canada's premier school of painters.

In the mid-1920's Franz Johnston resigned from the Group. A.J. Casson was named as his replacement. Later, in order to broaden their national base, the Group sought other artists, including Edwin Holgate of Montreal in 1930 and L.L. Fitzgerald of Winnipeg in 1932.

Their last exhibition before disbanding was in December 1931, at the Art Gallery of Toronto, now the Art Gallery of Ontario. Many of their works now reside there as well as in the National Gallery of Canada in Ottawa, and in the McMichael Canadian Collection in Kleinburg, Ontario, which is dedicated to the Group and opened to the public in 1966.

James Edward Hervey MacDonald

was born in Durham, England, on May 12, 1873. A founding member of the Group of Seven, he is best known for his paintings of the Algoma region of northern Ontario. One of his most famous works, *Mist Fantasy* (1922), now hangs in the Art Gallery of Ontario. Before dying in 1932 in Toronto, MacDonald made several painting trips to the Canadian Rockies, taught at the Ontario College of Art, and wrote poetry, which was not published until after his death. Some of his best-known paintings include *The Tangled Garden* (1916) and *The Solemn Land* (1921), both in the National Gallery.

Lawren Stewart Harris

was born into a wealthy Brampton, Ontario, family on October 23, 1885. He was the only member of the

Group not to have been a commercial artist. After university, he studied art in Berlin from 1904 to 1908. Returning to Canada, he painted in northern Quebec and did numerous architectural portraits in Toronto, where he became friends with MacDonald and Thomson. By the 1920's Harris had become an outstanding landscape artist and painted in the Algoma and Lake Superior regions before heading for the Canadian Rockies. In 1930 he even traveled to the Arctic to paint. Some of his best-known works include *North Shore, Lake Superior* (1926) and *Maligne Lake, Jasper Park* (1924), both in the National Gallery. More than others in the Group, Harris's works leaned to the abstract, and by the 1930's he had moved to the abstract school. He was an artist-in-residence at Dartmouth College in New Hampshire and helped found the Transcendental Group of Painters in Santa Fe, New Mexico, in 1939. He lived and worked in Vancouver, British Columbia, from 1940 until his death in 1970.

Alexander Young Jackson   was born in Montreal on October 3, 1882. Not only did he leave a rich legacy of paintings steeped in land-born nationalism, he eloquently presented the Group of Seven's philosophy in many articles and in his autobiography, *A Painter's Country*, first published in 1958. He studied and worked as a commercial artist in Montreal and Chicago before taking up serious study of painting in Paris. In 1913, feeling that his work was ignored in Montreal, Jackson moved to Toronto, where he became close friends with Thomson. Jackson shared his training in painting techniques and color, and Thomson shared his knowledge of the outdoors. Before the Group's first show, in 1920, Jackson had produced some magnificent landscapes, including *Terre Sauvage* (1913), *The Red Maple* (1914), and *Frozen Lake, Early Spring, Algonquin Park* (1914), all in the National Gallery. These, combined with his outspoken demeanor, gave him considerable

prominence. Twice he visited the Arctic, in 1927 and 1930, as he was eager to paint what he saw as Canada's unique climates and landscapes. Jackson died in April 1974, in Kleinburg, Ontario.

A Quebec Village *by A. Y. Jackson.*   National Gallery of Canada, # 1812, oil on canvas

Franklin Carmichael   was born on May 4, 1890, in Orilla, Ontario. He first encountered the Group's members in 1911 as an apprentice at Grip Ltd. He later continued his art studies in Antwerp, Belgium. On his return, he worked as a designer and continued painting landscapes of northern Ontario in watercolor and oil. His better-known works include *Autumn Hillside* (1920) in the Ontario gallery and *Snow Clouds* (1938) in the National Gallery. He taught at the Ontario College

of Art from 1932 until 1945, when he died.

Arthur Lismer

was born on June 27, 1885, in Sheffield, England. He studied art there and in Antwerp before beginning work in Canada in 1911 as a commercial artist, also at Grip Ltd., where he met other Group members. He later brought F.H. Varley, a friend from England, into the Group. His best-known work is *September Gale, Georgian Bay* (1921) in the National Gallery. But it was teaching that became his abiding career. He taught at the Ontario College of Art from 1919 to 1927 before becoming educational supervisor at the Art Gallery of Toronto until 1938. He ran the Montreal Children's Art Centre from 1941 to 1967, while also lecturing in Canada, Europe, and South Africa. He died in Montreal in 1969.

Frederick Horsman Varley

was born in Sheffield, England, on January 2, 1881. He studied art there and also in Antwerp. His friend Arthur Lismer encouraged him to emigrate to Canada in 1912. He worked as a commercial artist in Toronto until commissioned by the government in 1918 to record scenes of World War I in Europe. He executed several portraits and four large paintings, which were highly praised and brought much recognition. Unlike other Group members, Varley did not concentrate on landscapes. His first real passion was portraiture. In 1926, he moved to teach at the Vancouver School of Decorative and Applied Arts. In 1933, he and J.W.G. Macdonald, a Scottish painter, founded the British Columbia College of Art, which closed after two years, a victim of the Depression. Varley moved to Ottawa in 1936 and produced few paintings for two years until he traveled to the Arctic on a government supply ship. In 1944, he returned to Toronto, where he died in 1969. His best-known works include *Someday the People Will Return*, a war scene from 1918, now in the National Gallery; two landscapes, *Stormy Weather, Georgian Bay*

(1920) in the National Gallery and *The Cloud, Red Mountain, British Columbia* (1927–1928) in the Ontario gallery; and portraits, *Vera* (1930) in the National Gallery and *Dharana* (1932) in the Ontario gallery.

Francis Hans Johnston   (later changed to Franz) was born on June 19, 1888, in Toronto, where he met other Group members at work. While he painted with the Group in Algoma, he participated only in their first exhibition in 1920. He was uncomfortable with the controversy surrounding the Group's efforts at self-promotion, fearing it would hurt his own reputation as a painter. In 1921 he left Toronto to become principal of the School of Art in Winnipeg and, after resigning from the Group, returned to Toronto to teach at the Ontario College of Art. His best-known works from his Group paintings include *Fire-Swept, Algoma* (1920) and *The Fire Ranger* (1920), both in the National Gallery. Johnston died in Toronto in 1949.

Fueled by the energies of its immigrants, the developing values of its native-born, the innate natural majesty and richness of its land, and a growing self-confidence and appreciation of its bounty, Canada's imaginations are taking flight in all directions. There is a price to be paid in divisiveness for such determined diversity. But Canadians believe— they must, in order to maintain the national differentiation they feel so strongly—that the sum of their separate parts will be greater and stronger than any mix where the individual pieces are lost in a formless stew.

Not long ago, Robert Fulford, then editor of *Saturday Night*, said, "My generation of Canadians grew up believing that, if we were very good or very smart, or both, we would someday graduate from Canada." For today's generations of maturing Canadians, such thoughts seem increasingly strange.

The Economy

Who Runs Which Country?

It is entirely possible today that some average American works in his hometown in a skyscraper owned by Canadians in a downtown being redesigned by Canadians, processes office forms printed by Canadians, grabs a quick lunch in a restaurant owned by Canadians, buys a Canadian novel in a bookstore owned by Canadians, or watches construction of a new office tower being built by Canadians.

After work he jumps on a railcar made by Canadians and powered by electricity imported from Canada to meet his wife in a car built in Canada from Canadian iron ore to drive on Canadian cement to his home constructed with Canadian lumber, underwritten by Canadian financing, covered by Canadian insurance, and heated by Canadian natural gas to watch American programs with Canadian actors on a

Canadian cable TV system or to read a Canadian-owned newspaper printed on Canadian paper while listening to their favorite rock group, all Canadians.

The fictitious American family might go out to dinner at a luxurious Canadian-owned hotel or to a Canadian-made movie. On the weekend, if the weather coming down from Canada is good, they might take a Canadian-made bus to the seashore to a condominium they rent from a Canadian family. That evening they might sip some Canadian whisky or Canadian beer hauled south on an American railroad owned by Canadian investors. And while they are sleeping, their home could be burglarized by Canadian gangsters working the States for a few months.

It is a very important measure of the advanced state of economic integration in North America today that no one really pays any attention to this phenomenon, unique in a world just becoming aware of its acute economic interdependence. Two independent countries, each of which began national life as a collection of English colonies and then went its own way politically, have now drifted back together so closely economically that virtually every step any significant group takes has some kind of effect on both countries' economies and their differing dollars.

With a common border, a common culture and language, and a common capitalist tendency for profit, Canada and the United States have now forged the closest economic links of any two truly independent countries in the world. Every year they exchange more than $150 billion in goods, services, and resources, by far the largest exchange between two countries in the world and, for the United States, more than its combined trade with Europe and Japan. The United States trades more with the single province of Ontario than it does with the entire country of Japan.

About three quarters of Canada's exports and imports involve the United States. Even though the American economy is fully ten times

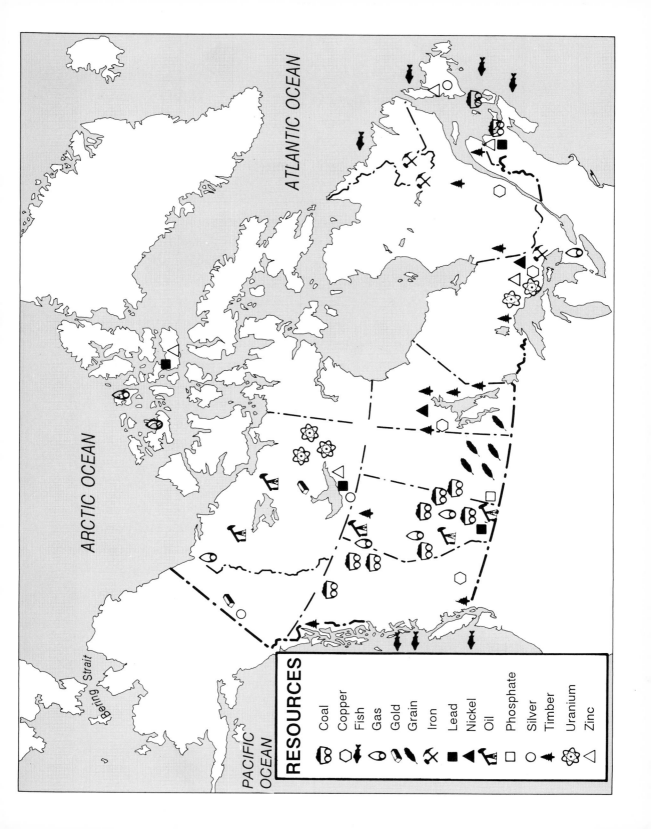

ARCTIC OCEAN

ATLANTIC OCEAN

PACIFIC OCEAN

Bering Strait

RESOURCES

Resource	
Coal	
Copper	
Fish	
Gas	
Gold	
Grain	
Iron	
Lead	
Nickel	
Oil	
Phosphate	
Silver	
Timber	
Uranium	
Zinc	

larger than Canada's, about one fifth to one quarter of American exports and imports involve Canada.

Free Trade

Despite a new Free Trade Agreement that began binding their economies even tighter in 1989, the two peoples remain only dimly aware of how closely intertwined their lives have become. Canadians have paid little attention to the increased jobs and other benefits that came from foreigners investing their money in Canada and close attention to any departure of any foreign operations. But Canadians always were acutely aware of how much their existence seemed to depend on events elsewhere—interest-rate decisions made in Washington, asbestos prices set in Germany, and even the weather in Florida, where frosts raise the price of Canada's winter vegetables. The Canadian identity, as several Canadian writers have noted, is darkly colored by the feeling that the end of the rainbow never falls on Canada. So certain are Canadians that difficult times lie just ahead that they are among the world's most heavily insured peoples.

But now the economies are developing such interdependence that the advantages and vulnerabilities go both ways—American automakers would be crippled without the many models and crucial parts produced under their separate contracts with Canadian workers. Many American urban areas wouldn't be rehabilitated without Canadian investors and financiers. And thousands of American workers wouldn't be employed without the new factories of Canadian companies.

Exporting Know-how   In a matter of years Canada, once the model of a country dominated by foreign investors, has itself become the fourth-largest foreign investor in the United States, behind only the

Netherlands, Great Britain, and Japan. In some sectors such as metals and machine manufacturing Canada is already the number-one foreign investor. And the United States is not the only target for Canadian money and ideas; Africa and Asia, especially the developing countries around the rim of the Pacific Ocean with their 1.8 billion potential

Manufacturing the United States Space Shuttle Arm was contracted out to Canada by NASA. It unloads, maneuvers, and retrieves space cargoes.   Canapress Photo Service

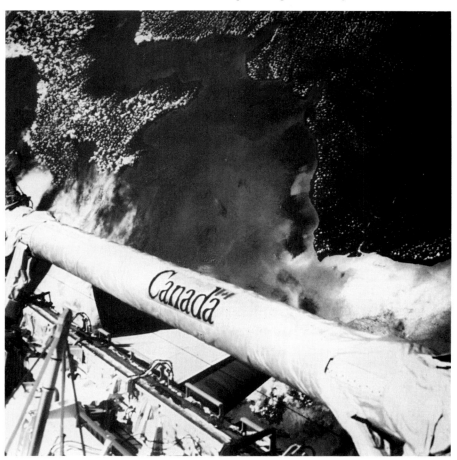

consumers, are encountering Canadian goods and investors.

Canadians, and their companies, have some major advantages in such lands. They speak French and English, the two most frequently used international languages. They have expertise in North American technology. But they have no association with any of the new countries' colonial past; in fact, Canadians can point out they were once a colony themselves. And while it is closely tied to the United States's economy, Canada has retained its political and cultural independence enough to stand alone in the eyes of other lands. As one Canadian businessman put it, "We export know-how, not a way of life."

Canada is the world's largest fish-exporting nation. This catch of herring is near Little Harbour, Nova Scotia.   Canadian Office of Tourism

Fur

Exporting knowledge is a far cry from the economic foundation of Canada. For centuries the country was little more than a vast repository of natural resources. The search for and mining of many minerals across Canada's breadth—the gold, lead, zinc, silver, asbestos, phosphate, uranium—would come later, providing wages for the workers, riches for the owners, and reasons for entire towns to spring up, flourish, and in some cases live on. But an initial driving force behind the exploration of Canada was a simple three-letter word: fur. Most of Canada is inhospitable to farming, so strewn is it with rocks and ponds, rivers and swamps, lakes and forests. But this same landscape combined with the harsh climate produces abundant wildlife, which nature clothes in rich fur.

Native North Americans had long used the skins for clothing and decoration. But the arrival of white traders opened up the whole European market. In exchange, the natives got muskets, knives, trinkets, and liquor. By 1700, France's fur empire stretched from James Bay in the north, up the St. Lawrence River, across the Great Lakes, which Louis Jolliet and Father Jacques Marquette explored for France in 1673, and all the way down the Mississippi River to the Gulf of Mexico. Their inland headquarters were Green Bay, Wisconsin, and Sault Ste. Marie at the northern tip of Michigan.

Company of Adventurers

But it was two disgruntled French traders, Pierre Radisson and his brother-in-law, Médart Chouart de Groseilliers, who carried their grievances to Britain and first alerted entrepreneurs there to the profit potential in Canada's furs. The result was the Hudson's Bay Company. Beginning in 1670 around the shores of Hudson Bay and later moving inland to fight off would-be rivals with a canny trading skill and a frontier ruthlessness, the company grew to become one of history's most powerful corporations. It eventually presided over a vast area that stretched from Hudson Bay across Canada's Arctic and prairies to the Pacific and down into what became Oregon. Forts of the Bay Company became Canada's cities and towns. At one point the company, whose British merchant investors never set foot in North America, ruled over much of what was to become the nation of Canada. According to *Company of Adventurers*, the first of a fascinating three-volume corporate history by Peter C. Newman, one of Canada's leading writers, the company's territory covered one twelfth of the earth's surface, an area ten times the size of the Holy Roman Empire at its height.

Now owned by Kenneth Thomson, a Canadian billionaire, the Bay lives on in Canada's cities as a major chain of department stores and, in many of Canada's isolated communities until 1987, when the Bay's northern operations were broken off and sold, as a general store and trading post. There native trappers and the store manager bargained over the price of a season's catch that was to make its way to the international fur auctions in Montreal and London.

National Policy

Canada's modern economic thinking and foundation were adopted in 1879 by the government of Sir John A. Macdonald, the first prime minister. Dubbed the National Policy, the bold plan involved building a transcontinental railroad, which would permit broad settlement of the Canadian West, and imposing strict protective tariffs. This meant that incoming foreign goods would artificially cost more than the equivalent Canadian product. And it thereby gave Canadian industry, which was and is located primarily in central Canada, a homefield sales advantage in a market of captive customers.

It was a policy that would come to be deeply resented in Canada's outlying parts because it treated them much like internal colonies, forcing them to buy goods from Ontario even though, without the tariffs, they could buy items for less money from nearby American regions. But the plan, wedding trade protectionism with deep government penetration of the economy, has shaped Canadian thinking—and fears—ever since.

Canada has always been short of two things—people and capital. To get most major undertakings under way, it has taken either government or foreign involvement. When the geographically more hospitable United States undertook to build its transcontinental railroad in the 1860's, it already had a market of 40 million citizens to help support it. When Canada finished the first of its two transcontinental railroads in 1885, the young country had only 4 million citizens. For reasons of national unity and security, Canada's federal government moved to get it built by offering the Canadian Pacific Railway $25 million, 25 million acres, a twenty-year guarantee against competition, and tax-free status for all its property forever.

American and Other Foreign Investors

Much of Canada's expensive early infrastructure—its sewers, power plants, railroads, and the like—were built with money borrowed from foreign investors, mainly British at first. Some still is. By the Great Depression of the 1930's, however, the payments were a heavy burden, both financially and politically. Officials decided then to encourage ownership by foreigners instead of borrowing from them. It was reasoned that when money was borrowed, repayments had to be made regularly to the lender in bad times as well as good. But a foreign owner would have to suffer in the bad times as well as enjoy the more prosperous days.

In those days, and especially immediately after World War II, no nationality was more eager to buy into Canada than the Americans, whose giant industrial base had been expanded by the war's demands but had suffered no damage from combat. And, as usual, Canada was happy for the investments, for the new jobs they created, and for the foreign trade they stimulated. With its relatively small population, Canada has had to be much more of a trading nation than the larger United States, which long had enough customers to satisfy even its biggest firms without seeking foreign sales. Canada still exports more than 25 percent of its gross national product compared with about 10

Building the Canadian Pacific Railway was a vital step in stitching together Canada's far-flung peoples. Taken in the early 1880's, this shot shows a railroad bridge in Elk, British Columbia. National Archives of Canada/Negative no. C 4545

percent in the United States. For instance, 61 percent of Canada's zinc goes overseas, 85 percent of its vast wheat harvest, and 88 percent of its newsprint production.

For American companies, Canada was a modest market close by. A branch plant there got them behind Canada's protective tariff walls. Historically, there has been little concern in Canada over corporate bigness; Canada's antitrust laws are without teeth and society in general has shown little of the basic distrust of large corporate empires that fueled the antitrust movement in the United States, where many empires have been broken up by government or court ruling. A Canadian base also made it easier for American companies to do business with other protected countries of the British Commonwealth. As usual, the major attractions were Canada's natural resources—the iron ore, nickel, wood pulp, newsprint, asbestos, lead and zinc, and, after major discoveries started in the late 1940's in Alberta, the oil and gas. Nearly 100,000 Americans had rushed into Canada's Yukon Territory in the great Klondike Gold Rush of the late 1800's, which was really an American gold rush on Canadian territory. But instead of drifting back home in a few years, the new American buyers of the mid-century stayed as owners.

Americans soon became, by far, the largest outside investors in Canada, owning 75 percent of all foreign-owned companies. This helped create many thousands of jobs many years before they might have been created by another Canadian company developing on its own. And it helped enable Canada to move more quickly than its southern neighbor had from a frontier society to a modern, industrialized welfare state. And due to its location beneath the security umbrella of the States, Canada did not have to support a huge self-defense budget. Instead, its governments, Progressive Conservative and Liberal alike, stressed social spending with, for instance, a broad national health insurance plan that insured everyone against daily and catastrophic medical expenses.

Years after many modern governments were encouraging birth-control programs to control their population growth, Canada's federal government was still encouraging families to have babies by paying bonuses at birth followed by monthly government support checks.

Foreign ownership, by paying taxes and creating jobs that created new taxpayers, helped support this intricate social welfare system. But for all its advantages, foreign ownership was also resented, and more deeply so as the twentieth century moved toward a close and Canadian self-confidence grew.

Immigrant Entrepreneurs

By 1967, when Canadians celebrated their 100th birthday with Expo, an international fair in Montreal, a new spirit of togetherness was infecting quiet Canada. Even Quebec's culture, which had long been Canada's most vibrant, if the most confined, was beginning to be recognized outside the country. Also, in the 1960's Canada took an important step that would echo through its society for decades. It greatly liberalized its immigration laws, opening the country's doors to millions of newcomers from all parts of the world. The country's previous policies had concentrated on recruiting educated new Christian citizens from northern European lands, which kept its foreign minorities to an almost invisible minimum. Now, suddenly Canada's cities, primarily Toronto and Vancouver, fairly exploded with the colors, cuisines, cultures, clothing, languages, and traditions of a score of new nationalities, many of them from Britain's other former colonies, now fellow members of the Commonwealth. One study in the late 1970's found that forty-five of every hundred residents in Toronto had been born in another country.

Now, in Toronto, property tax notices are routinely issued twice a year in six languages—English, French, Italian, Greek, Portuguese, and Chinese—to meet the needs of so many immigrants who may never learn English or French.

There have been frictions as old Canadian ways and rules meet traditions and expectations from even older foreign cultures. And such rampant diversity can create real problems of unity and so many differing demands on government. But there is in Canada a general atmosphere of acceptance and compromise, and the new cultures have produced a very vibrant, open society full of many flavors from the cooking to the thinking.

One of the major effects of this flood of new lifeblood has been an explosion of individual ambitions as the newcomers, unencumbered by Canada's quiet, resigned old ways of thinking, set about forging their own businesses, families, and futures. At the same time, Canada's population was passing the 26 million mark, small by global standards, perhaps, but sufficient now to support a national economy, instead of a collection of regional ones. Almost without noticing it, many Canadian companies had grown to become national in scale, too, with offices, factories, and sales in many corners of the country. In the simple old days of Canada's one-legged resource economy, a Newfoundland fisherman could not survive in Ontario. A British Columbia logger would have very little to do on Prince Edward Island. In those days Canadians' jobs defined their living location, and their geography defined their jobs. But this is an age of technology now, and the career horizons of that British Columbia woodworker's child need not be defined or confined by his or her father's. Computer technicians are needed everywhere. So modern job skills are far more portable than Canada's old ones.

The regular transfer of workers from one facility in one corner of the country to another in a distant province not only strengthened the worker's experience professionally but it broadened the entire family's perspective and exposed them to understanding fellow Canadians better. To help promote such education the federal government financed "foreign" student-exchange programs—among schools in various provinces. This was all a new, unifying experience and it began to give individual Canadians a sense of the scale and potential power of their country. This new kind of attitude was, in turn, reflected naturally in Canadian culture with an explosion of original plays and books, which thrived on the increasing number of citizens with higher educations. And it was also reflected in the economy, where consumers and companies had more money to spend.

More Power to You

One of the strongest forces drawing Canada and the United States closer together economically has been actually invisible. It is electricity.

Both countries need a lot of it. Both countries can generate a lot. But for new power the Americans must rely on coal or oil-fired generators, which pollute the air with their exhaust fumes, adding to the acid-rain problem in both countries, an increasingly prominent environmental concern. Acid rain occurs when natural rain falls through polluted air and washes the chemicals out into lakes and rivers below, affecting fish and other life there. Canada, which contains roughly one third of all the fresh-water supplies in the world, still has many undeveloped sites where vast amounts of power, called hydroelectricity, can be generated simply by letting the water fall from tall heights. It is cheaper and cleaner to do, and these sites are typically long distances from population centers, so environmental protests to these dams are few.

Some critical Canadian nationalists charge that Americans, thus, are exporting their power problems and manage to get Canadian power cheaper than Canadians do. But the political power of the resulting new construction jobs, the ensuing sales revenues in American dollars, and the operating efficiencies that accompany larger projects have always outweighed the criticisms.

These power sales and exchanges have been going on since the first transborder link in 1901 tied the Canadian Niagara Power Company Ltd. to its American corporate parent near Buffalo, New York. And one need not look far to sense some of the important ramifications of these ties. It was the failure of some Canadian relay switches in Ontario that set off the great power blackout of 1965 that crippled most of northeastern North America for many long hours one night.

Fortunately, the times of peak power demands are different in each country. In the summer, when American air conditioners are humming the loudest, consumption in cooler Canada is at its lowest, creating a surplus that can be transmitted south to hungry American power companies. In the winter, when Canada must work harder to stay warmer, it is the Americans who can ship surplus power to the north.

But with the continuing growth in power demands in both countries and the decline in popularity of nuclear generators in the United States, more power will likely be flowing south than north. Huge, long-term contracts worth billions of dollars have been signed between American electrical companies and the provincial power firms in Canada. These guaranteed contracts are then used by the Canadians to obtain cheaper financing for the vast construction projects that can include changing the courses of entire rivers and hollowing out of solid granite an underground generation chamber larger than a football field. But so strict are environmental regulations in Canada that besides building miles of dikes and blasting tons of stone, the construction crews on the mammoth James Bay project also had to see to carefully moving several families of beavers.

But still the links in Canada can be north-south, not east-west. Quebec Hydro alone now sells more than $1 billion a year in electricity to New England and New York. Manitoba sells ten times as much power to American states as it does to Saskatchewan next door.

And studies are even under way to harness the generating potential of the unusually high ocean tides in the Bay of Fundy between New Brunswick and Nova Scotia. Special gates would trap the high tides and then slowly let the water run out, using the natural flow of the ocean's twice-daily fall to low tide to produce the same power as sixteen nuclear generators at much less cost both financial and ecological. Much of the money to build this—and many of the resulting customers for the electricity—would be American, primarily in nearby New England.

Mega Corporations

One way Canadian corporations spent their money was to buy each other up. With no meaningful government regulations to stop them, Canada's corporate world went through a long consolidation process, which typically saw a few companies get very large in each economic sector. This constriction reduced competition, resulting, many believed, in prices higher than necessary. The new owners said the enlarged operations made them more efficient.

But the consolidation also created some powerful players with the expertise, the sales savvy, the financial resources, and the ambition to try some new areas. Having developed their home market to maturity, Canadian entrepreneurs were beginning to look elsewhere to fuel the kind of routine rapid growth they had come to expect as owners, shareholders, and workers in the new Canada. Nowhere was closer or easier than the United States. And Canadian investors sent their money and ideas streaming across the border.

New York City's Largest Commercial Landlord

Canadians have emerged as able, energetic competitors in many other sectors—real estate, construction, transportation equipment, insurance, manufacturing, telecommunications equipment, restaurant chains such as Hardee's, hotels such as the Four Seasons and Ritz Carlton, publishing, liquor and beer, retailing. Very quickly, the Canadian beers Molson's, Labatt's, and Moosehead jumped onto the list of top-ten American imports, which created more jobs and profits back home. Ironically, the New Brunswick beer Moosehead created a Canadian beer that was better known in the United States, where it was available in all fifty states, than it was in Canada, where it was on sale only in four of the twelve provinces and territories.

The Reichmann family, Jewish immigrants from Morocco who began by selling tiles in Toronto (and still do sell tiles), took their mammoth Olympia & York empire with interests in paper, oil, and real estate and quickly became the largest commercial landlord in New York City. They also owned major shares of American companies like the old Santa Fe Railroad, department-store chains, and large real-estate projects elsewhere, including London. Kenneth Thomson, whose father began business with a tiny radio station in northern Ontario, expanded the family's publishing empire from Canadian newspapers until he owned more than 110 American newspapers. Another Canadian investor, Conrad Black,

Rush hour in the subway, Montreal.   George S. Zimbel

owned four dozen more. Mortimer Zuckerman from Montreal bought and rejuvenated both the *Atlantic Monthly* and *U.S. News & World Report*. In an effort to diversify, a number of large Canadian firms bought controlling or significant interests in American companies. For instance, Joseph E. Seagram & Sons, the Montreal-based distiller and one of the world's largest, bought nearly one quarter of E. I. du Pont de Nemours & Company, the United States chemical giant. And Canadian Pacific, a giant corporation whose holdings include the Canadian Pacific Railway, got into the act, acquiring the United States' Soo Line.

National Banks   Canadian banks have a particular advantage.

There are usually around twelve federally chartered banks in Canada. But the top five—the Royal Bank, the Bank of Montreal, the Canadian Imperial Bank of Commerce, the Toronto Dominion Bank, and the Bank of Nova Scotia—control more than 85 percent of all the assets in Canadian banks. With their current size and national strength, these Canadian institutions give significant competition to American banks, which by law cannot be national.

"We see the United States as one of our major expansion areas in the years ahead," the chairman of the Toronto Dominion Bank said as he announced an increase in his bank's staff in the States. "We are realizing that we are North Americans, not just Canadians. And this is a North American market, not just a Canadian and a United States market." The Bank of Montreal felt the same, and bought up the large Harris Bank in Chicago.

"We used to be a large Canadian bank with international operations," the chairman of the Royal Bank has noted. "But now we are a large international bank with a strong Canadian base. There's a difference." Indeed there is. By the mid-1980's the Royal's foreign operations outside Canada produced more net revenues than its operations back home.

The new economic reality of the last few years of the twentieth century is that foreign trade between countries usually grows faster than the domestic economies by themselves. At the same time there is mounting fear in many lands—especially those like Canada, where foreign trade is a major fact of life and a major reason for prosperity—over protectionism. The fear grows because many other governments are coming under increasing pressure from domestic businesses to erect import restrictions, tariff barriers, and other rules and regulations that protect local businesses by discriminating against foreign competitors.

Indeed, this was an attitude once strongly shared by Canadians. Some still feel that way. But now that Canada's industries are strong enough to compete with the once-feared Americans abroad and at home, the government felt free to negotiate a special arrangement.

Two Irishmen Talk Trade

Beginning in 1984 the government of Canada was led by Prime Minister Brian Mulroney of the Progressive Conservative Party. Mr. Mulroney, arguably the first Canadian prime minister to rise from the working class, had numerous common interests and a good working relationship with the then American President, Ronald Reagan. Both were of Irish extraction, both were sons of working men (the prime minister's father was an electrician, the president's a shoe salesman), and, significantly, both had the confidence-building experience of leading successful business careers before entering national politics and being successful as conservative party leaders.

Canada is the only major industrial power with a domestic market of less than 100 million people. To survive, it must sell to other countries, primarily the United States. Concerned about Canadian companies being cut off from those American consumers someday, the prime minister suggested a free-trade agreement with the Americans. There are about 230 treaties and other agreements governing fisheries, commerce, wildlife, pollution control, transportation, and many other activities between Canada and the United States. This total includes the Automotive Products Trade Agreement of 1965, which, in effect, created free trade between the two countries in that important economic sector.

The larger free-trade talks began in May 1986. There was long, hard bargaining, complicated by the nations' geographic and emotional intimacy. Instead of being conducted in distant foreign lands, Canadian-U.S. talks occur in the local "neighborhood," as it were, with the affected civilian parties of both sides huddled right outside the negotiating room. These Canadian-U.S. talks are similar to, say, a City Council meeting where it takes only a few minutes to vote on a new, multimillion-dollar housing project but several weeks of debate to increase the fee for dog licenses, because so many people are directly affected. Nonetheless, agreement was reached on this historic trade pact on October 3, 1987, and it was sent to the U.S. Senate and the Canadian House of Commons for ratification.

Two Nations Without Barriers   The agreement repeals all customs duties between the two countries. It reduces nontariff barriers and various government and industrial regulations that served to make it harder for foreign goods to compete locally. And it created an entirely new, nonpolitical mechanism for settling any trade disputes that arise. There are hundreds of pages to the agreement, but basically it phases in over a ten-year period virtually unlimited access to the Canadian economy for goods and most services for the same guaranteed access to the larger American market for Canadian businesses, and creates in the process a joint North American market of more than 270 million people, large enough to compete efficiently with other emerging vast trade blocs such as the European Community.

But while the U.S. Senate ratified the treaty almost unanimously in August 1988, the road to approval was considerably more troubled in Canada and revealing about some of that country's vital concerns. Prime Minister Mulroney had called for elections to the 295-seat House of Commons for November 21 of that year. The 52-day election campaign became not so much a voter evaluation of the Conservatives' four years in power, but a virtual referendum on the free-trade agreement. John Turner, then the leader of the Liberal Party, and Edward Broadbent, leader of the small, socialist New Democratic Party, seemed to strike a raw national nerve by their charges that Mr. Mulroney had sold the country out to become, in effect, the 51st state of the United States. To observers of Canada, this was a familiar fear. And, historically, it had been a potent one, having helped destroy several governments who dared to talk of opening Canada.

Big Fish and Little Fish
To be sure, some of the 1989 concern was purely political and perhaps desperation; opinion polls had shown the Liberals trailing the Conservatives. But while understanding the economic advantages, a good number of Canadians were genuinely worried that in order to compete on the hard, fast track with American companies, Canadian companies and their workers would have to sacrifice some of the costly social values and programs they prize. "There is a very deep-seated feeling in the pit of every Canadian's stomach," said Ken Dryden, the attorney and former all-star hockey player with the Montreal Canadiens. "This feeling is an anxiety that when you live beside a place as big as the United States, no matter how much you may like or admire it, you must keep it at arm's length lest you eventually be consumed by your friend."

"We have tremendous differences," added Pierre Sarrazin, a writer and movie director. "In Canada, we stress the tribe more, not your rampant individualism. We finance a huge social security net; yours is more every-man-for-himself. We fear being sucked into your values and lifestyle."

"If we become basically one North American economy with you," Mr. Dryden told one interviewer, "we'll be forced to make economic decisions solely on the basis of competition. And I wonder if values like our collective Canadian compassion can survive those pressures."

"We don't fear competition!" Mr. Mulroney emphatically countered his critics. "We seek it out. We can compete with the best of the world." Obviously, in the privacy of the voting booth, enough Canadians agreed with him to provide an overwhelming majority in Parliament.

Controlling 170 of the 295 seats in the new House of Commons, Mr. Mulroney easily won approval of the free-trade treaty in December 1988. And the pact took effect a few days later, on January 1, 1989. Though the government's popularity plummeted over new taxes, the trade pact was so popular in many sectors that within 90 days, Canadian and United States officials were back at the bargaining tables to speed up some of its provisions.

A Mature Canada

The new trade agreement augured even closer economic integration in the years to come as customers and large and small companies on both sides of the border became more accustomed to making decisions based on opportunities in their far-larger joint market of North America. But for many, Canadian voters' decisive rejection of fearful protectionism and their confident acceptance of the challenge of competition was of equal historic importance as an economic gauge of the country's emerging maturity, even if someday Canada was to see a grumbling Quebec go its own independent way.

Bibliography

Nonfiction

There are numerous other sources for students seeking more information on Canadians, their country, and their lives. Two national histories are basic, thorough, and available in paperback. They are:

Canada: A Story of Challenge (revised edition) by J.M.S. Careless. St. Martin's Press (New York) and Macmillan of Canada (Toronto), 1974.

The Pelican History of Canada (revised edition) by Kenneth McNaught. Penguin Books (New York; Harmondsworth, Middlesex; Ringwood, Victoria, Australia; Auckland, New Zealand; and Markham, Ontario), 1976.

Thomas B. Costain wrote a history of the French rule in Canada, which should remain in many libraries. It is *The White and the Gold: The French Regime in Canada*, Doubleday Canada Ltd. (Toronto), 1954.

Peter C. Newman has written a compelling three-volume history of the Hudson's Bay Company, one of the world's oldest ongoing business firms. The books, especially Volumes I and II, describe in intimate detail what life was like for the trappers and traders opening North America for development in their scramblings for furs on the harsh continental frontier, especially Canada's north and west. These highly recommended books are:

Company of Adventurers, Vol. I, Viking Penguin (New York; Harmondsworth, Middlesex; Ringwood, Victoria; Auckland, New Zealand), 1985.
Caesars of the Wilderness, Vol. II, Viking Penguin, 1987.
Merchant Princes, Vol. III, Viking Penguin, 1990.

Another helpful set of historical books was written by Pierre Berton. They include: *The Invasion of Canada, 1812–13*, Penguin (New York and Toronto), 1988, about the military invasion of Canada by United States troops during the War of 1812; *The National Dream: The Great Railway 1871–1881*, Penguin (New York and Toronto), 1989, about building the transcontinental Canadian Pacific Railway; *Klondike Fever: The Life and Death of the Last Great Gold Rush*, Alfred A. Knopf (New York), 1985, about the gold rush in Canada's Yukon Territory; *The Arctic Grail*, Viking Penguin (New York and Toronto), 1988, a recounting of the opening of the Arctic by Canadian and American explorers; and *Why We Act Like Canadians*, McClelland and Stewart (Toronto), 1982, an examination of Canada's national personality.

For a detailed description of how Canadian society and business works, I recommend two volumes by Peter Newman: *The Canadian Establishment*, Seal/McClelland and Stewart Ltd. (Toronto), 1977, and *The Acquisitors*, McClelland and Stewart Ltd. (Toronto), 1981. A new Newman volume is due out in 1993. And I would also suggest *Controlling Interest: Who Owns Canada?* by Diane Francis, Seal Books/McClelland-Bantam (Toronto), 1987.

On Canada's complex relationship with the United States, there is *Life with Uncle: The Canadian-American Relationship* by John W. Holmes, University of Toronto Press (Toronto, Buffalo, London), 1981.

Both the Canadian and American governments have also published many documents and reports on their relationship, most recently including the free trade agreement that took effect in 1989. Canadian consulates in major U.S. cities often keep such data in small reference libraries open to the public. The Canadian Embassy in Washington and its consular offices in Chicago, Los Angeles, New York, and other major cities across the United States maintain a library of government publications and official information, which can be invaluable for research papers and is often free. Because of the large volume of requests, however, students must be as specific as possible when seeking information.

Three such government publications that are particularly helpful are *The Canada Handbook*, an annual paperback collection of facts, figures, and descriptions of Canada and its life; *The Canadian Indian*, published by the Ministry of Indian Affairs and Northern Development (Catalogue No. R32-76/1986E); and *The Inuit*, published by the same ministry (Catalogue No. R32-75/1986E). Statistics Canada is a helpful government agency that collects data on all aspects of Canadian life.

For more general information and observations on Canada, I would recommend: *A Nation Unaware: The Canadian Economic Culture* by Herschel Hardin, J. J. Douglas, Ltd. (Vancouver), 1974; *Sometimes a Great Nation: Will Canada Belong to the 21st*

Century? by Peter C. Newman, McClelland and Stewart Ltd. (Toronto), 1988; and *The Canadians* by Andrew H. Malcolm, Paperjacks (Toronto), 1987. This book is also available in a French edition from Presse de la Cité, Paris, 1987. A videotaped network television documentary based on the book is available through CTV Television Network, Office of Air Sales, Marie Baccari, 42 Charles St. East, Toronto, Ontario M4Y 1T5, Canada.

For insights on the life and remarkable thoughts of a Canadian professional hockey player, the best book is *The Game* by Ken Dryden, Penguin Books (New York), 1984, and Collins (London), 1984. Mr. Dryden and Roy MacGregor also wrote *Home Game*, McClelland and Stewart Ltd., (Toronto), 1989, a fascinating look at the central role of hockey in the lives and hearts of Canadians.

For current affairs and essays, the most helpful periodicals would be the *Globe and Mail*, a daily newspaper published Monday through Saturday in Toronto (444 Front St. West, Toronto, Ont. M5V 2V5, Canada); *Maclean's*, a weekly newsmagazine published by Maclean-Hunter Ltd. in Toronto (777 Bay St., Toronto, Ont. M5W 1A7, Canada); and *Saturday Night*, a monthly magazine (36 Toronto St., Suite 1160, Toronto, Ont. M5C 2C5, Canada).

Fiction

In fiction, perhaps the work best known to students is the *Anne of Green Gables* series by L. M. Montgomery, Bantam Books (New York), 1983, and Watermill Press (Mahwah, N.J.), 1985, which has also become a series of TV movies.

For a taste of one of Canada's greatest modern writers, students might also try *The Papers of Samuel Marchbanks* by Robertson Davies, Elisabeth Sifton Books/Viking (New York), 1985, which are the observations and social commentaries of a fictitious friend of Mr. Davies's.

Farley Mowat is another modern Canadian writer whose written works, concentrated heavily on man, nature, and their relationship, have also been turned into motion pictures, most recently *Never Cry Wolf*, Seal Books (Toronto), 1963, a popular Walt Disney movie about a scientist who studies Arctic wolves by living amongst them; and *The Dog Who Wouldn't Be*, Atlantic-Little, Brown (Boston/New York), 1957, about a dog who is not interested in his family roots.

Other works include: *Angel Square* by Brian Doyle, Groundwood Books (Toronto), 1987, in which a child growing up in postwar Ottawa learns the absurdity of racism through his own friendships; *Whiteout* by James Houston, Greey de Pencier Books (Toronto), 1988, in which a 17-year-old travels to the Arctic alone and learns much about native life—and himself; *Who Is Francis Rain?* by Margaret Buffie, Kids Can Press (Toronto), 1987, about a youth who, seeking to escape domestic bickering at home, comes upon a dangerous and mysterious island; *False Face* by Welwyn Katz, Groundwood Books (Toronto, 1987, in which a 13-year-old discovers some ancient

Indian artifacts and some personal and ethical problems; and *Shadow in Hawthorne Bay* by Janet Lynn, Lester & Orpen Dennys (Toronto), 1986, about a girl who emigrates from the Scottish Highlands to the Canadian wilderness in search of relatives, and herself.

Also recommended are: *Underground to Canada* by Barbara Smucker, Clarke, Irwin (Toronto), 1977, published in the United States under the title *Runaway to Freedom*, Harper & Row, (New York), 1978, about the flight of two black girls from slavery in Mississippi to a new life in St. Catharines, Ontario; *Blood Red Ochre* by Kevin Major, Doubleday (Toronto), 1989, in which tragedy unites a white boy and an Indian youth, each on a separate search; *Scrubs on Skates* by Scott Young, McClelland and Stewart (Toronto), 1985, in which one of the town's best youth hockey players is suddenly transferred to the worst team and he learns how true success can only come through teamwork; *Hannah* by Robina Salter, McClelland and Stewart (Toronto), 1986, about a young woman's career as a traveling nurse in rural Newfoundland.

The Scorched Wood People, McClelland and Stewart (Toronto), 1977, and *The Temptations of Big Bear*, McClelland and Stewart (Toronto), 1975, both by Rudy Wiebe and both in paperback, provide stimulating insights into the lives and thoughts of Canada's native peoples.

And no study of Canada or of Canada's writings would be complete without reading—and better yet, hearing—the poems of Robert Service, a young Briton who spent many years in Canada's wild and woolly Yukon Territory in the nineteenth century at the time of the great Klondike Gold Rush. By day he worked as a bank teller. But during those long northern nights, his mind and frigid fingers turned to writing some of the most evocative verse about human beings on the frontier of civilization. They are considered classics and available in most anthologies.

The most popular of Service's poems include "The Cremation of Sam McGee," "The Shooting of Dan McGrew," "The Quitter," and "The Spell of the Yukon." Under the sponsorship of the Canadian government, Tom Byrne, an Irish actor, has studied the life, character, and writings of Service, whom he brings to life and portrays each summer day at Service's old cabin in distant Dawson City. Enthralling 60-minute tape recordings of Mr. Byrne's readings are available for $11 (U.S.) from Tom Byrne Tapes, 664 Hawkes Ave., Vancouver, British Columbia V6A 3J1, Canada.

Filmography

The Canadian Film Distribution Center (CFDC) at the State University of New York at Plattsburgh makes available to American educators educational films and videos produced by the National Film Board of Canada, the Quebec Ministry of Communication, and other Canadian producers. A free catalog, describing over 800 titles, is available upon request from the CFDC. They also have a separate catalog of materials available to teachers of French and others with a special interest in French Canada. For further information, contact the Canadian Film Distribution Center, Feinberg Library Room 126, SUNY Plattsburgh, Plattsburgh, NY 12901; (518) 564–2396.

The National Film Board of Canada has recommended several films, available in a variety of formats, of specific interest to teachers and young adults:

Rendezvous Canada, 1606 (29 min; part of the History Re-enactment Series; available in 16mm or VHS). Re-creating the lives of two teenagers from radically different cultures, this film highlights the native Canadian way of life prior to contact with Europeans.

The Sweater (10 min, 21 sec; available in 16 mm or VHS). An animated version of a short story by Roch Carrier, set in the rural Quebec of his boyhood. The author recalls the passion for playing hockey that he shared with other boys of his community. This film won awards at Canada's major film festivals and at film festivals in New York and London as well.

City of Gold (21 min, 40 sec; available in 16 mm or VHS). A vivid recollection of the Klondike gold rush at its height, this film captures the agonizing months during which would-be prospectors tried to reach Canada's fabled gold fields, 2000 miles (3,200 kilometers) north of civilization. Other scenes show Dawson City during its frenzied days. This film won awards at the London, Cannes, and Edinburgh film festivals, and was nominated for an Oscar.

Ikwe (57 min; available in 16 mm or VHS; part of the Daughters of the Country series). In a remote area of North America in 1770, an Indian girl is given to an ambitious Scot as part of a trade agreement. She quickly learns her husband is insensitive to the ways of her people. She leaves him when smallpox ravages her village.

The Wake (57 min, 51 sec; available in 16 mm or VHS; part of the Daughters of the Country series). Joan is a typical single parent of the 1980s. But her people are American Indian, considered inferior by the white townspeople. When Jim, a young white police officer, displays rare compassion for some of her relatives, Joan is moved. Although a relationship develops between them, a tragic event makes Joan realize the differences between their two worlds.

The two films above, along with two others in the Daughters of the Country series, *Places Not Our Own* and *Mistress Madeleine*, have been praised at film festivals in North America.

For home use only, Incredible Manitoba Animation has produced a number of animated short films by Academy Award-nominated animators Richard Condie and Cordell Barker, including *The Big Snit*, *Getting Started*, and *The Cat Came Back*.

Some of these films, along with a number of others, make up the National Film Board of Canada's Short Film Festival. For more information on any of Incredible Manitoba Animation's available short films, call Whole Toon Access, (206) 391–8747.

The New York City office of the National Film Board of Canada can provide additional listings and information, as well as order numbers for the films they distribute. Write the National Film Board of Canada, 1251 Avenue of the Americas, New York, NY 10020 or call (212) 586–5131.

Index

Numbers in *italics* refer to illustrations.